"A message the world needs to hear."

Edi Osborne

Founder of Mentor Plus – Adviser to the profession – Author of *Firm Forward* – USA

"This book is the shot in the arm that every small accountancy firm needs to get the inspiration to aspire to bigger and better things."

Heather Townsend

Author of *The Go-To Expert* and *The FT Guide to Business Networking*
– Adviser to the profession – UK

"A ground-breaking work of research from which accountants and business owners can all benefit."

Colin Dunn FCA

Director and Chief Innovation Officer, Panalitix – Author of
Accountants: The Natural Trusted Advisors – Australia

"At last, a book that solves the self-confidence crisis within the profession. It will change your perspective forever. And is essential reading for any accountant looking for the confidence to succeed."

Simon Chaplin

Founder of Socks Up Simon – Award winning practicing accountant
– Adviser to the profession – UK

"This is an enormously powerful, stunning and profoundly important book. It's a massive contribution to any firm, irrespective of size. And here's what you must do with it: make sure everyone (yes everyone) in your office has it. Make sure everyone (yes everyone including you) takes two days off to read it, re-read it AND highlight the crucial things to them. Then re-group, go through everything you've highlighted and agree to do it — right now. You'll become an amazing firm in amazing time. It's as stunningly simple as that."

Paul Dunn

Founder of B1G1: Business For Good – Adviser to the profession
– Author of *The Firm Of The Future* – Singapore

"What The World's Most Inspiring Accountants brings to the profession is on a par with what Jim Collins and his team have delivered with books such as Good to Great. It's a must-read page-turner that I couldn't put down, and I can't imagine an accounting firm anywhere in the world that would not benefit greatly from learning the lessons it contains."

Mark Lloydbottom
Author of *Deeper: Advanced Practice Management Strategies*
– Adviser to the profession – UK

"A truly inspiring book, acknowledging the role accountants play in society, which often goes unnoticed. The book highlights some of the simple day to day things accountants do, which make a significant difference to their clients and the communities they serve. This should inspire all accountants to acknowledge their own stories and to learn from firms who are no different from them, yet have been able to demonstrate the inspiration they bring."

Bridgitte Kriel
Project Director: Practice, South African Institute of Chartered Accountants – South Africa

"A brilliant book that provides the missing key for accountants struggling with value pricing. It shows accountants the real value of what they do, inspires them to do even more of the things that make a difference, and gives them the confidence to price accordingly. Reading it makes me incredibly proud and excited to be an accountant."

Mark Wickersham
Author of *Effective Pricing for Accountants* – Creator of Cloud Pricing
– Adviser to the profession – UK

"It is so useful for accountants to read about the techniques, processes and tools firms use to assist clients with business improvement. It is clear helping clients focus and use the latest cloud tools, leads to significant improvements."

Thea Foster FCA
Founder of The Added Value Corporation Pty Ltd – Adviser to the profession – Australia

"Before I started working alongside accountants with Satago, I honestly didn't know what they actually did most of the time. But this book reveals the truth, and perfectly illustrates the power of accountants to make a real difference to the strategy, growth and cashflow of small businesses, and to the lives of the people running them."

Dr Steven Renwick
Founder of Satago, software for turning sales invoices into cash – UK

"Progressive accountants can—and do—change lives. This book is proof of that and is inspiration for any accountant or business advisor who wants to extract greater meaning (and not just greater profits) from what they do. Transforming accountants into change agents for business owners is why we exist and what drives us at PARADOX. We're rapt to see a number of the firms we've advised regarding their strategy and modern marketing approaches amongst the ranks of inspirational accountants whose stories are shared here. Be the leader your business clients are silently begging for. Don't wait to be asked. Lead. They'll follow."

MC Carter
Founder of PARADOX – Adviser to the profession – Australia

"This book categorically proves that accountants really can make a difference."

Ken McManus
Head of Practice Support at The Institute of Chartered Accountants of Scotland – UK

"Put this pioneering book at the top of your reading list AND your re-reading list. Why? Because in 2016, all the talk is about 'content' marketing. There's no more powerful content to market in professional services than how an accounting firm improves the lives of their clients. And this book contains the most powerful examples ever likely to be seen in print of how profoundly business owners can be helped by you to reach their aspirational goals."

Martin Bissett
Founder of The Upward Spiral Partnership – Adviser to the profession
– Author of *Passport To Partnership* – UK

"Illustrates the 4 Cs (Commitment, Courage, Capability and Confidence) the profession needs to be future ready. Let it challenge and inspire your thinking."

L Gary Boomer

CEO Boomer Consulting – Adviser to the profession – USA

"A must-read book with a crystal clear message. Accountants can make a profound difference. Make a difference to yourself, your firm and your clients. Its message is also compelling; you and I can do it one client at a time, one piece of advice at a time, one piece of work at a time.

In these heart-warming and authentic stories you will find practical applications and inspiring insights that will open your eyes to see that the 'ordinary' things we do as accountants can have an extraordinarily positive, sometimes life changing, impact on the lives of others. Read it and be inspired. Reflect on it and become convinced. Act on it and change your work and your world."

David Oliver

Founder of Insight Marketing and Senior Exec at MyFirmsApp
– Adviser to the profession – Author of 14 books – UK

"We all learn from experience. We learn what clients like and value from the reactions we get from our clients. This book enables you to learn from other accountants' experiences. To really understand what clients like and value about the service they have received.

I defy any accountant in practice to look through this book and not find new ideas as to how to better serve clients, inspire their teams and grow their firms. The AVN team have collated many truly inspiring stories from accountants across the globe. And these are set out in an easy to read style. You can go through them in order or just dip in and out.

No matter what size practice you run, from sole practitioner upwards, you will find practical, inspiring and replicable ideas and initiatives throughout this book."

Mark Lee FCA

Founder of BookMarkLee.co.uk – Consultant Practice Editor at AccountingWEB.co.uk
– Adviser to the profession – UK

"Normally accountants in practice play down their vital role in the world of business. But this remarkable book clearly demonstrates how accountants make life better, one business at a time, one extra pound of wealth at a time, one extra job at a time. And it proves that accountants everywhere can do the same. So it's definitely an inspiring must-read for the profession and for ambitious business owners everywhere."

Paul Shrimpling
Founder of Remarkable Practice – Adviser to the profession
– Author of *Bamboo Marketing* – UK

"A brilliant, ground-breaking summary of the best of the best in the profession today. Any accountant who doesn't read this book, or sits on their hands after reading it, needs their head examining."

Amy Harris
Co-Founder of CrunchBoards, all-in-one forecasting and reporting engine software – UK

"Finally a book that proves accountants can guide their clients on a journey of transformation and help them to achieve their goals. It also reveals the simple keys to building a truly inspirational firm that really makes a difference, instead of getting caught in the trap of just providing information."

Steve Major
Founder of Pricing Power – Adviser to the profession – Australia

The world's most inspiring accountants

Steve Pipe, Susan Clegg
and Shane Lukas

First published 2016 by Added Value Solutions
7 Midland Way, Derbyshire, S43 4XA

This edition published 2016

A catalogue for this book is available from the British Library

Typeset by Steven Levers, Sheffield

Printed and bound in the UK

ISBN 978-0-9551007-6-5

This book is dedicated to the
inspirational accountants featured within
these pages and to the many others who
have inspired us over the years.

Contents

Brief inspirational stories

Chapter 1

Introduction

Practicing accountants across the world are making an impact that is quite simply extraordinary in its range and scale.

Their economic impact could probably have been predicted. But what has not previously been fully appreciated is the profound impact accountants are also having on a personal, social and emotional level.

Indeed, the research here suggests that, apart from the medical profession, there is probably no other group making such a big difference to the lives of so many people. And certainly not to their businesses.

Research that will change the way you view accountants

On these page you will:

- Read 62 stories from accountants on every continent
- See how they are generating growth, creating jobs and changing lives
- Understand how they are making the world a happier and fairer place
- Discover the four main types of services accountants provide that make all of this possible
- Debunk the 15 excuses that prevent some accountants achieving their full potential
- Learn how to build an accounting firm that is extraordinarily rewarding for everyone involved, both financially and emotionally.

Who should read it

This book has primarily been written for professionals working in accounting firms across the world. By helping them to understand the profound impact they can have, we hope it will inspire them to stand tall, inspire them to serve their clients better, inspire them to make more of a difference and inspire them to improve the reputation of the entire profession.

As such it is relevant to the accounting profession's leaders of today (founders, partners, directors etc.), the leaders of tomorrow (managers, qualified accountants, trainees, students etc.) and anyone else who cares about the profession.

We also hope it will inspire businesses and the wider community to:

- Understand the many ways that accountants can make a profound difference
- Find and work with an accountant who does the things that will help them achieve their goals
- Recognise, appreciate and give credit for the difference accountants make
- Support accountants as they explore new ways to be even more valuable
- Challenge accountants to do better when they are underperforming

How it will help you as an accountant

The insights on these pages will help you:

- Identify the things you can do that clients really value
- Understand the (often profound) difference you can make to their businesses and their lives
- Refocus your efforts on the things that have the greatest impact
- Generate bigger fees from your existing clients – by doing more of the things they value
- Improve your marketing – by collecting your own inspiring stories, and using them to communicate the benefits of working with you more clearly
- Win high quality new clients – who choose you because you are doing these things
- Earn higher prices – because you are doing more of the things clients really value
- Recruit the best and most talented team members – who are inspired by your story, because as one of them in this book puts it, "today's best young graduates want to join businesses where they know they will make a difference doing worthwhile work."

As a result, they will also help you to:

- Build and run a more successful practice – with better clients, better fees and a better team

- Transform your work-life balance – because having better clients and better fees means you will earn more in less time, and having a better team means you can delegate more

- Live a more joyful and fulfilling life – with the emotional rewards that come from making a real difference and receiving sincere thanks

- Leave a lasting legacy – by making life better for your clients and colleagues, their families and communities

About the inspiring firms featured

You are about to read 62 stories from 57 firms in 8 countries. And when you read them you will see clearly why every single one of those firms deserves to be included.

But obviously they aren't the only firms doing inspiring things. We know there are many others who also deserve recognition.

The reality is that these 57 represent the accounting profession as a whole.

They represent it in the sense that they prove that accountants everywhere can and do make a profound difference. And also in the sense that they are representative of the vast majority of the global profession in terms of size, structure, client and location.

For example, the 57 firms featured:

- Are predominantly small firms – with 71% having one or two partners or teams of less than 10 people

- Come from every continent in the world – Europe, Africa, Asia, Australasia and the Americas

- Serve clients of every type and size – although most of them are the same type of small and medium sized businesses that every other accountant also serves

- Are run by accountants with all types of backgrounds – from school leavers to corporate big hitters, young mothers to the almost retired

- And even include recent start ups

And since there is clearly nothing unique about them, if they can do inspiring things, so can every other accountant in the world.

IMPORTANT NOTE: The story chapters quantify the financial impact accountants are making using whatever currency each firm used when telling us their stories. However in this introductory chapter we have converted their many different currencies into US dollars for clarity and simplicity.

The profound difference accountants are making

Because they only feature a few dozen firms, the 62 stories in this book barely scratch the surface of the contribution accountants across the world are making.

Even so, this very small sample of the profession has helped to generate ALL of the following economic success:

- 19 businesses saved from extinction
- 4 new businesses launched – one of which grew to $5 million in 24 months
- 562 jobs created or saved
- Sales increases of 33%, 169% and, in one case, $2.8 million
- Profit increases of 142%, 273% and, in at least one case, over $1 million
- Turn losses as big as $150,000 into profits as high as $900,000
- Transform cashflow – in one case turning $450,000 of borrowing into $950,000 positive cash balances
- Win better customers and charge better prices
- Make it possible for one business to invest $300,000 in new equipment to improve productivity
- Raise $2.2 million to fund a management buyout and future expansion
- Lift a client out of "special measures" and back into mainstream banking
- Give employees a pay-rise for the first time in five years

At a personal level their impact has included:

- Improving work-life balance – in one case an entrepreneur's workload was slashed from 80 to just 10 hours a week

- Helping several clients own their dream homes – including one overlooking the sea on a beautiful Greek island

- Preventing several other clients from losing their homes

- Restoring family harmony – and preventing business disagreements tearing a family apart

- Helping an exiting entrepreneur to pass on his business in a way that secured his own financial future, and created exciting new opportunities for the management team

- Restoring the self-esteem of a son who thought he was going to lose the business his father had worked so hard to build

- Obtaining an extra $375,000 insurance payout for an Alzheimer's sufferer

- Making it possible for a young business owner and his wife to adopt a child

- Generating the funds to pay for expensive medical treatment

- Preventing financial blackmail ruining a client's business and life

- Dealing with a client's end of life financial issues, so that he and his wife could make the most of their last few precious days together

- Keeping a business going while its founder coped with life-threatening cancer

- Transforming the lives and prospects of junior team members, by helping them to "step up" in their careers

- Turning their clients' business and personal dreams into reality

- Giving them a new sense of purpose and worth

- And in several cases, also turning them into millionaires

Importantly, the research also proves that accountants are having a profound social impact. For example, the 62 stories on these pages include evidence of:

- $1.375 million of cash raised for worthy causes

- 225,000 hours of help provided on a pro bono basis

- At least two charities founded by firms of accountants – one of which has already saved 550 young girls in Cambodia from sex trafficking

- $420,000 of grant funding raised to prevent a much needed community facility closing, and

- The lives of 9,653,329 people in need being made a little bit better by accountants using www.b1g1.com to connect with, and "micro-give" to, causes that resonate with them

And remember, all of those impacts have been made by a very small number of firms with a very small number of clients.

Imagine how staggeringly large the impact is when the numbers above are multiplied many thousands of times over to reflect what hundreds of thousands of accountants are doing for many millions of their clients.

The emotional impact

However, even these kinds of staggeringly large numbers don't tell the whole story.

As part of the research we also identified the emotional impact. And as Table 1 shows, the transformation in how clients feel before and after their accountant's input is every bit as profound.

How they are doing it

The inspirational stories on these pages reveal in precise detail the hundreds of things that accountants have done to help achieve these kinds of results.

And from analysing those stories it appears that there are four main ways that accountants are making a difference:

1. Core services – the things that every accountant already can and must do

2. Advanced services – the things every accountant must now be building into their plans

3. Specialist services – the things most accountants can adopt a "just-in-time" approach with

4. Humanitarian services – the extra things that make life joyful and really set accountants apart

Table 1: How people felt before and after their accountant helped them

BEFORE - How they felt before being helped by an accountant	AFTER - How they felt after being helped by an accountant
Tired	Relieved
Burned out	Proud
Daunted	Secure
Stressed	Happy
Vulnerable	Calm
Overwhelmed	Confident
Frustrated	Focused
Disillusioned	Positive
Disheartened	Optimistic
Demoralised	Grateful
Nervous	Excited
Worried	Weight has been lifted
Anxious	In control
Confused	Able to dream big again
Running blind	Peace of mind
No idea why things were going wrong	Delighted
Like hamsters in a wheel – running round and round and getting nowhere	Fantastic
	Thrilled
On an emotional rollercoaster	Ecstatic
Sometimes they even felt:	
Scared/terrified (for example that they would lose their business and, more importantly, that their families would suffer by losing their homes)	
Paralysed	
Ashamed	
Rock bottom	
Devastated	
Depressed	
Hopeless	
Guilt and inadequacy	
Like a "moron"	
Suicidal	

Core skills and services

The really good news is that the vast majority of the difference accountants are able to make appears to come from their core skills and core services – i.e. the things that every accountancy practice in the world should be capable of doing.

Some of the most valuable core skills include asking the right questions, understanding what is most important to the client, listening, building trust, communicating effectively, and being supportive and encouraging at the same time as being truthful and candid.

While the core services that create the greatest impact include:

- Accounting systems – to deliver up-to-date, reliable and accurate information at all times
- Robust internal controls – to minimise the risks of things going wrong
- Bookkeeping support – to ensure the integrity of the underlying accounting data
- Training – so that bookkeeping and accounts systems are used properly
- Management accounts – so the business leaders receive the information they need
- Decision support – so that information is properly understood and used to make better decisions that lead to better results
- Virtual Finance Director – to give business owners proactive high-level input when they need it
- Acting as a sounding board for ideas, issues and challenges – to give business owners an independent second opinion
- Board/Management meeting attendance and support – to keep business owners focused, efficient and effective
- Business plan creation – to help clients move forward in carefully thought through ways
- Integrated profit and loss, cashflow and balance sheet forecasting – to ensure that their plans stack up financially
- Recommending books, software, third party experts etc. – to expose business owners to the very best ideas, tools and support
- Proactive tax planning – to capitalise on legitimate tax reduction opportunities

- Defensive tax planning – to challenge excessive claims made by the tax authorities

- Cashflow management – to ensure clients don't run out of cash

- Debtor (receivables) collection – to prevent bad and slow paying debts derailing the business

- Raising finance – to fund growth, investment and other plans

- Cost and profitability analysis – to support better product, sales and marketing decisions

- Buying and selling businesses – to help clients achieve their strategic plans

- Exit/Succession planning – so clients can get out when they want, and on the terms they want

Of course, what constitutes a "Core" service probably varies from country to country. And is also likely to evolve over time. In Australia, for example, several of the Advanced services described in the next section have already become Core because the market there is so dynamic.

Cloud accounting is another prime example. A few years ago this would probably have been regarded as an Advanced or even Specialist service. But as the case studies in the book illustrate, it has become so widespread, important and transformationally powerful that it must surely now be regarded as a Core service by any accountant who wants their practice to have a future.

One of the practitioners in the book summarises it all brilliantly this way:

"The point is that what we accountants see as fairly ordinary advice and support can often make an EXTRAORDINARY difference to the businesses, lives and happiness of our clients. The profession has so much more power to do good than it gives itself credit for. That power is at our fingertips. And thanks to new technology, such as cloud accounting and everything that goes with it, our power to make a difference is getting greater and greater by the day."

Another puts even more succinctly: "To us accountants it probably all seems very simple and basic, but to clients it can make a profound difference."

Advanced services

Advanced services are the things that every accountant must be building into their plans. Mostly because they allow you to make much more of a difference. But also because many accountants are already delivering them, and those that don't keep up will get left behind.

The inspirational stories in this book suggest that this category of Advanced services includes:

- Goal setting
- Strategic planning
- Business coaching and mentoring
- Workflow and business process automation
- Systemisation
- Pricing advice
- Growth advice
- Profit improvement advice
- Benchmarking
- KPI identification, measurement and monitoring
- Grant finding
- Family finances – which includes family financial forecasting, retirement planning and other personal financial planning

A few years ago some of the things on the above list would have been regarded as Specialist services. And in a few years' time some of them will probably even be regarded as Core services, such is the change within the profession.

Many firms are developing their competence in these areas through training or by buying in specialist software and tools. Others are recruiting people who already have the necessary skills (for example, many practices are recruiting tech-savvy young people to deliver their cloud based automation services). And some firms are forming strategic alliances with third parties who can deliver Advanced services to their clients on a sub-contract or revenue sharing basis (for example, strategic alliances with an ActionCoach for business coaching services etc.).

Specialist services

Specialist services are the unusual technical and commercial oddments that crop up from time to time. In the inspirational stories on these pages they materialise in the form of things as diverse as understanding obscure tax legislation and personality profiling.

The good news, however, is that most accountants can largely ignore these. They are probably best addressed on a just-in-time basis should the need for them ever arise. At which time, of course, the best approach may simply be to bring in a suitable third party expert to help out.

Humanitarian services

Humanitarian services are what really set accountants apart. They involve doing things which, at first sight, do not appear to be commercially "necessary". Examples include:

- Going the extra mile for team members

- Giving time and support to local good causes

- Fund raising

- Establishing charities and other not-for-profit initiatives

- Joining a movement such as www.b1g1.com to connect with like-minded businesses and support people in need around the world

- Encouraging clients to also do these things

Interestingly, though, on closer inspection, these humanitarian services are commercially sensible too. In particular they help accountants:

- Win new clients – by differentiating themselves as genuinely socially responsible

- Improve client loyalty – by proving that they really care

- Improve productivity – by giving their teams a greater sense of purpose and worth

- Improve service – by inspiring and motivating their people to go the extra mile

In addition, many accountants say that it brings them real joy to know that they have made life better for other people.

The rewards to accountants

Accountants who make a difference by delivering these kinds of services are rewarded extraordinarily well. For example, the financial rewards include:

- "In return we can charge higher fees, making it a win-win all round." – Mike Ogilvie, OBC The Accountants

- "Earned us our largest ever fee." – Andrew Gray, Kirkpatrick and Hopes

- "We now spend three times what we used to with our accountants and it's worth every penny!" Martin – client of Urquhart Warner Myers

- "[Our approach] gives us a great reputation and attracts a lot of new clients." – Pieter Esterhuizen, LUMENROCK

While on an emotional level, the rewards include:

- "It's so fulfilling knowing that we are part of something that is making a real difference." – Simon Maddox, Owadally & King

- "To have a purpose beyond our daily working life is both humbling and satisfying. To have that purpose together as a team is unifying and empowering." – Craig Stanmore, Jaques Stanmore Financial Group Pty Ltd

- "After all, if you don't enjoy it, what's the point?" – Ingrid Edstrom, Polymath

Accountants need more self-confidence

One of the alarming findings of our research was how reluctant accountants were to put themselves forward for inclusion in the book. Partly, of course, this can be explained by modesty, client confidentiality and them not fully understanding the legitimacy and integrity of the project or the authors.

Another possible explanation is that accountants aren't actually making a difference. But we simply we do not believe that is the case. All our research and experience during this project, and elsewhere, screams out to us that the overwhelming majority of accountants really are doing things that make a very real difference.

The problem is that most accountants don't properly understand the value and impact of what they do.

As a result they lack self-confidence. They say things like "we are ONLY accountants". And the truth about what they really are – a tremendous force for good – remains largely hidden.

Value pricing

That lack of self-confidence probably also explains why so many accountants struggle with value pricing. After all, the first rule of value pricing is to understand the value to the other party of what you are doing for them.

Our hope, however, is that the stories in this book will make it easier for accountants to earn a good living, because they will help you to:

- Recognise, understand and believe in the real value you already bring to clients

- Get your whole team focused on delivering more value by doing more of the things that make a real difference

- Recognise the importance of collecting and sharing stories of the value you bring and the difference you make – so that your clients also properly understand your contribution

- Charge prices that allow you to share in more of the value you deliver – which you can either do by value pricing, or simply by increasing your fixed prices or hourly charge rates

And now for the excuses

Together the authors have over 50 years experience of working exclusively with accountants, and two of us are even married to accountants. As a result, we know how much the profession loves to find excuses.

Some readers will probably have already started to come up with their excuses for why they can't be more inspiring and why they can't make more of a difference. So to save those readers time, here is a list of the most common excuses, along with the reasons why no true professional can use them:

1. **"It's too difficult"** – No it isn't. The stories in this book prove beyond doubt that most of the things that make a profound difference are actually very simple, and very easy for any accountant.

2. **"I am not good enough"** – Rubbish. If you are a professional, you are good enough. And if you are not a professional, you should not be in practice.

3. **"Our team are not good enough"** – Because it isn't difficult, if you have a professional team then they will be good enough. And if you don't have a professional team, the best way to find and recruit people who are good enough is to inspire them with your plans to make more of a difference.

4. **"It won't work / That is impossible"** – The inspiring stories in this book prove it is possible and that it works. That is the whole point.

5. **"It won't work in our part of the world"** – Yes it will. And the proof is simple… the inspiring stories here come from practices on every continent in the world.

6. **"It won't work for a firm of our size"** – The ideas have also been proven to work by firms of all sizes, including 42 with 10 or fewer team members (including recent start ups), and 16 larger firms, including regional, national and global players.

7. **"Our clients are different"** – In what way exactly? Do they not want more successful businesses, a better work-life balance, less stress, more money etc.?

8. **"Our firm is different"** – Of course it is. But so is every firm in this book. And if they can do it, so can you. The only question that matters is not whether you can, but whether you will.

9. **"We can't afford it because our prices are too low"** – So increase them.

10. **"We would lose all of our clients if we increased our prices"** – No practitioner since the beginning of time has ever lost all of their clients in this way. But, of course, you may lose some clients. So the question that really matters is this: will enough of your clients stay at your new prices? Happily, all the evidence suggests that firms lose very few clients when they charge more, and fewer still of their good clients leave. What's more, you will probably want to lose some of your most price sensitive clients, since that is how you free up the time to start focusing on making more of a difference. And very soon that new focus will also start winning you extra work and high quality new clients.

11. **"We don't have the right type of clients"** – You are either right or wrong with this assertion. If you are wrong, then you have no excuse! And if you are right, and you really do have low-grade clients, consider what that is telling you: i.e. what you are currently doing is only good enough to attract low grade clients to your firm. If you are happy with only having low grade clients, fine. But if you would prefer to have better quality clients, then your only logical option is to change what you do in order to become more attractive to better clients.

12. **"There are some other important things we need to do first"** – What could possibly be more important than serving clients better, and generating better results for you and your family? Certainly not redecorating the office, redesigning the website, installing new cabling and all the similarly shameful excuses that other firms make for doing nothing.

13. **"We will do it, but not now"** – The brutal truth is that you are kidding yourself. If you put off acting on the ideas in the book 'for now', you are in reality putting them off forever, since the half-life of enthusiasm is always very short and there will always be other "more important" things in your in-tray.

14. **"We tried that once and it didn't work"** – Logically, negative examples don't really prove anything. For example, if I were to pick up a Stradivarius violin and try to play it, sadly you would not hear sweet music. But just because I can't get it to work, doesn't prove that it doesn't work. In fact, all it proves is that I haven't currently acquired the skills and knowledge to make it work. Everything in this book has been proven to work by accountants just like you. So all you have to do is acquire the skills and knowledge to make them work for you too.

15. **"We don't have the tools, skills or knowledge"** – Well get them then! They aren't difficult to obtain, and the inspiring stories along with the free resources in Appendix 1 will point you very clearly in the right direction.

How to use this book

The inspirational stories are presented in alphabetical order of firm name. As a result, once you have read the three short introductory chapters, you can dip in and out of the rest of it in any order you like. Or, if you prefer, you can read it cover to cover.

Either way, our advice is as follows:

- Make sure you read it all – there are so many powerful insights littered across the pages that you really can't afford to miss any of them

- Treat it as a work book rather than a library book – use a highlighter pen to identify the bits that resonate most with you, and annotate your thoughts in the margins

- Draw up a list of key insights and potential actions as you go along

- Share the book with everyone in your practice – so that they all understand the difference accountants can make, and are all inspired to make even more of a difference themselves

- Arrange a meeting with your entire team to discuss their reaction to the book – and the implications for your firm

- Draw up an action plan – with complete clarity over who is responsible for each action, and the date by which it must be done

- Give someone the job of holding you accountable to make sure that the things on your action plan are actually completed

- Get your whole team collecting stories about the difference your firm has made

- And start sharing those stories with all your team members, clients, contacts and prospects

Free implementation resources

Appendix 1 contains details of the free implementation resources we have created to accompany this book, along with other free resources we think you will find useful.

They have not been included within the book itself so that we can keep them up to date and relevant to you regardless of when you are reading this. So please do request them. And please make the very most of them.

A quick word about "Full" and "Brief" stories

There are two types of stories in the book: "Full" and "Brief". But it is important to note that the distinction between them has nothing to do with the quality of the story.

"Full" stories are simply more detailed, and most of them have a standard structure, with standard headings guiding you through that structure.

"Brief" stories, on the other hand, are shorter: usually because they are intrinsically less complicated and can be told more succinctly, or they don't really fit the standard structure of a full story.

We believe that both types of stories are equally inspirational.

A manifesto for the accounting profession

The evidence is crystal clear. Accountants can make a profound difference. In fact you already are. You just need to do more of it. One business or person at a time. One decision at a time. One impact at a time.

So here is a five part manifesto and mantra to help everyone in your accounting firm do exactly that:

1. **WE CAN** – Believe in yourselves, because the evidence proves that as accountants you can make a profound difference.

2. **WE SHOULD** – Commit to work together to make more of a difference to more people, because it is the right thing to do, will make life better for you and others, and will make the world a better place.

3. **WE MUST** – Provide services that make a difference. And equip yourselves with the tools, knowledge and skills you need to communicate and deliver them.

4. **WE DO** – Grow your reputation, client base and team by telling others true stories about the difference you are making by doing what you do.

5. **WE PROSPER** – Grow your profits and wealth by pricing in a way that reflects and allows you to share in the difference you are making.

Chapter 2

Key lessons from accountants

Some of the most valuable parts of the stories in this book are the lessons accountants and their clients have learned along the way. In this short chapter, therefore, we have drawn together a small selection of the most insightful and inspiring "in their own words" quotes from accountants.

It is easy to make a big difference

"Lots of small actions can make a huge difference to a business and the life of its owners."

James Hellyer – Accountancy Edge

"The point is that what we accountants see as fairly ordinary advice and support can often make an EXTRAORDINARY difference to the businesses, lives and happiness of our clients. The profession has so much more power to do good than it gives itself credit for. That power is at our fingertips. And thanks to new technology, such as cloud accounting and everything that goes with it, our power to make a difference is getting greater and greater by the day."

Jason Blackman – Just Pure

"The great thing about harnessing cloud technology is that it frees up the time we need to be able to be a lot more proactively valuable."

Jody Padar – New Vision CPA Group

"I believe the profession is at a crossroads. Some accountants are helping customers integrate and automate things, improving accuracy and reliability, saving time and reducing costs. And others seem to be happy allowing their clients to limp along with legacy technology and systems that are slow, inefficient, costly and error prone. The first group are enabling economic progress, growth and prosperity. And not only are we proud to be part of it, but for the good of the profession we urge other accountants to join it too."

Sian Kelly – Inform Accounting

"A KPI monitoring and discussion approach is the key to deeper and more mutually rewarding relationships with clients."

Andrew MacDonell – BDO

"As accountants we obviously help our clients understand the numbers. But we shouldn't underestimate the importance of the role we also play in giving them moral support, reassurance, self-belief and confidence."

Niraj Pande – Auroma Accounting

"To us accountants it probably all seems very simple and basic, but to clients it can make a profound difference."

Claire Priestley – Clarand Accountants

"Our approach is always based on the fundamental belief that one of the keys to creating sustainable success is not only to facilitate the necessary changes, but also to teach our clients what we are doing. We empower them by giving them the knowledge and know-how to keep driving their businesses forward."

Brad Koehn – Berberich Trahan & Co

"We often don't appreciate the enormous difference we can make just by bringing people together and encouraging them to get their issues out onto the table. That alone can be profoundly valuable to them."

Jody Padar – New Vision CPA Group

"While I still talk to my clients about the importance of saving and planning for the future, I also tell them that they have to live for today because none of us has any idea of what's around the corner. We want to help clients get to a position of loving what they do. Creating businesses that they love and enjoy going to. But that they can also get away from when they want to. So they can go on their holidays, lead their lives and get the whole work-life balance thing perfect. And all without getting grief from an accountant who says negative things like 'you shouldn't be spending that money on holidays and enjoying yourself!'

The bottom line is that we don't want miserable clients. In the past, we saw too many people save all their money for retirement. And then something drastic happened, and they never got the chance to enjoy the fruits of all that hard work. It can be a tricky balance, of course. But it's probably the most valuable and important thing any accountant can do for their clients. Because that way we can help them to live lives without regret."

Kylie Anderson – RJS Accounting

"Because there are so many issues that businesses face, and so many potential ways of tackling them, they often have no idea where to start. So we believe that a key part of our role is always to help them to focus on and prioritise the quick wins, low hanging fruit, and the things they are really good at. That way they will get the best return on their investment of time and effort."

Dan Schmidt – EBCFO

The financial rewards

"We make a difference by giving [clients] 'the right information - to make the right decisions – at the right time'. And in return we can charge [them] higher fees, making it a win-win all round."

Mike Ogilvie – OBC The Accountants

"As well as making life better for our client's entire family, this exercise earned us our largest ever fee. And because what we did is so replicable, we now offer it as a packaged service to all of our clients."

Andrew Gray – Kirkpatrick and Hopes

"Our caring culture has undoubtedly been a key ingredient in our success. Because of it we have an incredibly loyal team, who really care about delivering the five-star service that gives us a great reputation and attracts a lot of new clients. In addition, their willingness to always go the extra mile for us and our clients has also allowed us to deal with inevitable stresses and strains on our resources, systems and structure that have been caused by our rapid growth."

Pieter Esterhuizen – LUMENROCK

"There is often so much untapped potential in people. And by giving it a chance to flourish we can make things better for everyone."

Ian Woollard – Pearson Bulchholz

The emotional rewards

"Every day I look forward to working with our amazing team, always searching for new ways to improve the lives of our clients and ourselves."

Jeff Kelly – LiveCA

"Today's best young graduates want to join businesses where they know they will make a difference doing 'worthwhile work.' And that's why I am so excited about building my career at a business that thinks that way too."

Jonny Pipe – intern at Northern Accountants

"If I'm honest, I was getting a bit stale. But now I really look forward to coming to work. It's so fulfilling knowing that we are part of something that is making a real difference."

Simon Maddox – Owadally & King

"To have a purpose beyond our daily working life is both humbling and satisfying. To have that purpose together as a team is unifying and empowering."

Craig Stanmore – Jaques Stanmore Financial Group Pty Ltd

"Making a genuine difference is joyful, uplifting and inspiring. It gives the entire practice a greater sense of purpose, a greater source of energy, and a greater feeling of happiness. And it brings practitioners, their teams and their families an immense feeling of pride."

Steve Pipe - Accountants Changing The World

"After all, if you don't enjoy it, what's the point?"

Ingrid Edstrom – Polymath

Chapter 3

Key lessons from clients

In this further short chapter we have drawn together a small selection of the most insightful and inspiring "in their own words" quotes from the clients featured in the rest of the book.

Making life better for clients

"Before, I felt I had failed my family. Now, I have the time, money and energy to support them properly."

Abdul Aziz – client of AA Chartered Accountants

"The impact has been profound in every single area of the business; this goes way beyond mere financial reporting."

Client of PH Accountancy

"I wanted to make my family proud of me. And thanks to my accountant, they really are."

Emma Savage – client of Pillow May

"Having a really good accountant has been instrumental in turning our dreams into reality."

Ann – client of Clear Vision

"It brings such joy to me, my team, my family and my nine-year-old son to know that we really are making a difference. So it's one of many things that I can't thank [our accountants] enough for. They really have changed my life."

Karen Ormerod – client of RJS Accounting

"What made it all work so well was having someone who actually cares about the future of the business, our strategy and our personal goals, as well as our business goals. I didn't know all of that was possible from accountants, as I thought it was just a numbers thing. But now I realise it's much more than that."

Alice – client of Clear Vision

"There's a renewed sense of energy and passion now, and that's all down to the commitment and support of our accountant."

Simon Barlow – client of Middel & Partners

"Having [a good accountant] is like having a business partner who I can bounce ideas off at any time. She explains all the financial data and reasoning behind her recommendations, but I am still in control of my decisions."

Emma Savage – client of Pillow May

"For the first time I've been able to go on holiday. I've lost a lot of weight and I'm actually a new person. Very positive, very calm, and in a very, very good place. And it's great to get out of bed and go to work knowing that I'm really going to enjoy the day."

Janine – client of Clear Vision

A quote to end all quotes

"I am no longer stressed. Why would I be? I have financial security for me and my family, a successful business, happy customers, and my dream home in the sun. What's more, the business is run brilliantly well by my team, and the management buyout we are working towards will ensure its future. So life is fantastic. Really fantastic. And to say I am proud would be an understatement.

We definitely wouldn't have achieved all of that without the tireless help of our accountants. They have focused and challenged us, provided a sounding board, kept us accountable, forced us to confront the key issues, brainstormed and suggested solutions, helped us to think big, ensured we took action rather than hiding behind excuses, prevented us making mistakes, and always made sure that the numbers stacked up.

In fact, and I never thought I would hear myself say this, but the more I think about it the more I realise it is true... my accountant has changed my life."

Chris Holt – client of Bartfields

Making life better for accountants

"Spend more on your accountant. It's worth it because low levels of fees mean low levels of support and a lack of attention to the business."

Nigel Botterill – client of Tayabali Tomlin

"The more money I spend with [my accountant] the more money I make."

Gavin Esberger – client of Northern Accountants

"This was my first experience of working with an accountant who looks to the future, not the past. And by saving our business and our homes, they have literally changed our lives. As a result we now spend three times what we used to with our accountants and it's worth every penny!"

Martin – client of Urquhart Warner Myers

Full inspirational stories

From working 80 hours a week to just 10 – the incredible difference this accountant made

A sole practitioner with a team of four based in Peterborough, England who has helped a client:

- Obtain £200,000 VAT refund within a week of submission
- Increase net profits by 142%
- Reduce his working hours from 70-80 to just 10 per week
- Reduce debt by £128,000

"Before, I felt I had failed my family," the client says. "Now, I have the time, money and energy to support them properly."

Background information

Adam's Cash & Carry Ltd is based in Peterborough and supplies food and other products to the catering trade. The company founder, Abdul Aziz, started the business in 2001 out of frustration with the poor service he had from his suppliers when he owned a fast food outlet himself. He had a clear vision of what a great supplier should look like and a driving ambition to succeed.

The situation at the start

Abdul attended a seminar run by AA Accountants in December 2011, with a presentation by Steve Pipe on "How to get an extra £2 million from your business". At that time he had recently moved the business to a 2.67 acre site with a 30,000 sq ft warehouse, all on a much bigger scale than his former premises.

- Debt was out of control, cashflow was poor, as was the credit rating of the business, and suppliers were not willing to extend credit terms.

- The new site had cost £1m + VAT and the business had had to fund the £200,000 VAT element of the purchase themselves. Their accountant at the time had told them it would take 3-4 months to reclaim the VAT and having such a large sum locked up had put the business at risk of closure.

- The business needed to invest in a large commercial freezer at a cost of £200,000 + VAT but the bank had declined to offer further funding as had other third party lenders. The freezer was critical to the business as without it they could not store the frozen produce that formed the bulk of the products they offered. This was another challenge to the viability of the business.

- Profit margins were around 11% and Abdul couldn't see any way to improve them. He was convinced that the only way to gain and retain customers was to keep his prices low.

- The business relied on Abdul for all decision-making, so he was working for 70-80 hours each week. As well as the impact on the efficiency of the business, his home life was seriously affected as he had very little time to spend with his wife and family.

- There were also huge issues with Abdul's employees due to the lack of targets, unclear job roles, a lack of accountability and a poor team culture.

- Customer care was weak and there was no complaints procedure for customers.

- The book-keeper at the time was unreliable and did not appreciate what the business needed in terms of financial information. "He made lots of errors and took up too much of my time," Abdul says now. This lack of management information was partly to blame for the bank's refusal to extend or increase the overdraft.

- Abdul felt he was paying too much tax as others in his industry were telling him this, but his accountant had never suggested any form of tax planning. This was causing further cash flow issues.

- The business lacked a clear vision. Although Abdul knew that he wanted to be successful, he did not have crystal clarity on what success meant in both tangible and intangible terms. His team certainly had no idea of the vision or the mission of the business.

The "How to get an extra £2 million from your business" presentation opened Abdul's eyes to the potential within his business and he immediately started work with Shaz Nawaz of AA.

How their accountants helped

The most pressing issue was the VAT refund that had put the business in jeopardy. Shaz worked with his contacts at HMRC, submitted the VAT refund prior to the end of the VAT quarter and negotiated the refund within a week of the submission. As Shaz says, "Getting a refund within a week of the VAT return being submitted is literally unheard of!"

The new premises had been bought from a large corporate and they had initially valued the plant and machinery at £1. Shaz liaised with a capital allowances specialist and entered a claim for £269,444. After long and protracted negotiations the claim was successfully agreed, and resulted in a very big tax saving.

Once these big issues had been dealt with, Shaz began a thorough overhaul of the entire business:

Systems for increased efficiency and better team culture – Shaz comments, "We had carte blanche to introduce as many systems as necessary to improve the efficiency of the business. Through working with us, Abdul had experienced at first-hand the benefits of having robust systems and processes and he knew that this was the way for his own business to run smoothly and efficiently in his absence.

"We built and developed a new team culture, one which was focused on outcomes and results. Client care was the number one priority and we worked diligently with the team to improve this.

"In addition we worked through the whole business structure, implementing systems for sales and marketing, client grading, referrals, admin duties, efficiencies, team management and every other area of the business. This resulted in the team working more cohesively and customers were delighted as they received a consistent and improved service."

This freed up much of Abdul's time to focus on other things apart from the day to day running of the business.

More profitable pricing – Benchmarking the business against the competition showed Abdul that it was possible to achieve higher margins. He was persuaded to increase his prices, on a step-by-step basis. The results were clear almost immediately – a 19.2% increase in his gross margin ratio. The actual gross profit, in monetary terms, increased by 109%.

The sales team began to systematically target a higher proportion of the 'diamond' grade customers, as these were the most profitable, and they developed a specific 'diamond' client care programme. High margin products that weren't selling well also became the focus of a cross-selling initiative.

Increased overdraft – Shaz set up a meeting with himself, Abdul and the bank manager to discuss increasing the overdraft. He compiled a succinct One Page Business Plan alongside a projection and cash flow statement to demonstrate how the business would service the overdraft and improve its financial standing.

"The bank manager was extremely impressed with our plans and our professional approach to assisting our client," Shaz says. "He agreed the increase in the overdraft, and due to being so impressed with our approach, he also became an introducer to our firm, referring his contacts to us."

Tax savings – Shaz arranged two meetings a year with Abdul (one pre and one post-year end) to discuss remuneration and corporation tax planning. Using AVN tax planning software, he was able to show Abdul all the options for extracting profits from the business so he could make the best decision and plan for the future. With some additional advanced tax planning, Abdul saved £15,000 in one year alone.

Better financial information – As the management information was so weak, Shaz arranged for one of his team to work in the business one day a week as the company's finance director. This meant initially arranging and supervising the training for one of Abdul's team and then implementing regular reviews of the financial statistics for the company and the production of management accounts.

Clarity of vision, mission and goals – The One Page Business Plan helped Abdul to clarify what he wanted from the business and how he defined success in measurable terms. Shaz explains, "We held strategy sessions with the senior team to get their input and their buy-in and worked with the whole team to gain clarity on the purpose of the business. From there we developed a clear mission for the business and by focusing on where they wanted to be in 3 and 5 years, the senior team members were able to help articulate the vision. We then agreed on SMART goals to help the business achieve its vision and mission."

The difference it made

- The biggest change has been to Abdul's work-life balance. His working hours have reduced to just 10 each week and even then he says that it's not really working, just catching up with his team and meeting customers.

- The impact of this on his family life has been enormous. Abdul can now spend much more time at home with his wife and children, so everyone is happier and less stressed. His son had long held an ambition to be sales manager of the business, but Abdul had always felt he was too inexperienced. With an external training programme and additional support from Shaz, he was made sales director in January 2015.

- Over the three years of working with Shaz, the business has seen turnover increase by 104%, gross profit margins increase by 19% and net profit increase by 142%.

- Shaz has helped Abdul to utilise his large site by leasing out car parking space. He also advised him to add some storage containers. "These can be rented to his customers on an annual agreement. They benefit through savings on bulk buying and he sells even more products to those customers for them to store in the containers!" Aside from the initial cost of buying the containers, the total rental income is pure profit. This means that in 2016 the net profit will increase by 109% excluding the normal annual increase from profits generated by additional sales, cross selling, efficiency etc.

- Debt has reduced by £128,763.

- 12 additional jobs have been created and, with a huge investment in team development and training, many existing team members have been promoted to senior roles.

- Customer feedback scores have risen from an average of 6.6 to 9.1. Customers are spending more, more customers have developed into diamond (i.e. top grade) clients, the business gets more referrals and customer retention rates and lifetime value have improved.

How it made them feel

"Excellent!"

This is the word Abdul uses to describe his life now – a very long way from the hopelessness he felt before he started working with Shaz.

As well as the success of the cash and carry business, he has been able to fulfil his ambition of becoming a property developer. Shaz has helped him to purchase eight new properties and to develop a piece of land to build 20 flats. And even more excitingly, he has also started flying lessons with the aim of becoming a pilot.

AA has been able to utilise the full range of their knowledge and expertise to support Abdul, and has brought in all the AVN tools and software to assist them. "It's been a hugely satisfying experience," Shaz says. "We've charged a five figure fee for our services and Abdul has been happy to pay that because he could see the ROI almost immediately. The hard numbers speak for themselves, but we all like to see the human side of success too, as, ultimately, this is more important than the numbers. What all this proves is that when you apply the processes the numbers will work for you and the effects can and will have a profound effect on the lives of those involved."

Coping with the sudden death of a young founding director

Abacus Accountancy is a four person firm in Braintree, England which has helped a client:

- Cope with the sudden and tragic death of a founding director who was solely responsible for the financial side of the business
- Restructure the accounting function to cope with her loss
- Continue to operate the business efficiently
- Continue to focus on the core business

"A lot of the support we've received has been emotional and confidence building – not just financial," says the client.

Important note

Unlike most of the chapters in this book, the story below has not been written by the authors. Instead, it was written in ready-to-publish form by the clients themselves.

Background information

The Phoenix Partnership (TPPE) is an education business partnership organisation that delivers services to schools and colleges to support Work Related Learning. We are a micro (i.e. two director/employee) business based in Essex. Our core services are 1) brokering and maintaining links between employers and their employees and education providers, and 2) facilitating and delivering student facing activities that develop employability and enterprise skills.

We are a for profit organisation, although the business has an ethos and core values that are more social and community enterprise in nature.

The situation at the start

TPPE was established by three directors (Mark Sexton, Maria Ramsey and Anne Page). In 2012, however, Maria resigned as a full time employee to pursue other interests, although she maintained her directorship and continued to assist the business by keeping the financial records, issuing invoices and by being the primary operator of the company bank accounts.

In late 2014, Maria suffered a stroke followed by a pulmonary embolism, and tragically passed away on Christmas Eve.

Although her fellow directors had taken over her crucial duties immediately she fell ill, Maria still had significant knowledge and as the main contact between the company, our bank and Abacus Accountancy, we needed to retrieve information and set up processes that would enable the company to function efficiently.

How their accountants helped

Paul and his team at Abacus immediately arranged for the remaining directors, Anne and Mark, to get up to speed with the 'books' and also helped to retrieve and update the company financial records. Mark's wife Jacci was 'recruited' to step in to manage the process and Abacus provided all the training she needed to understand their cloud based accounting software.

They even invited her into their office for a day, sat her on a spare computer and showed her how to use the system – all completely free of charge!

Abacus has provided on-going telephone and personal support to Jacci since she was appointed. It's been a total team effort, and they are always willing to go the extra mile to help us out.

The difference it made

They took all the stress out of the financial side of the business, allowing Mark and Anne to support Maria's husband over the New Year, and beyond.

Abacus advised TPPE on how to settle the Directors Loan Account in Maria's name. They helped Jacci to learn about the books very quickly and taught her how to reconcile the accounts with the bank records and how to pursue overdue invoices. This allowed Anne and Mark to carry on with the company's core business.

All the relevant paperwork was filed on our behalf and they were incredibly sympathetic towards the situation we had found ourselves in. They really helped to ease the pain during this stressful time.

How it made them feel

Maria's initial illness and sudden passing was obviously a shock to all. As Maria was by some years the youngest member of the team we were completely unprepared for this eventuality and therefore we felt nervous about how to ensure that we stayed compliant with HMRC and Companies House. Abacus helped us to overcome these worries and went above and beyond in helping us – even contacting us outside of office hours to reassure us and take the strain.

They have continued to support us, and have even helped put us in touch with outside advisers so that we can secure our growth plans over the next few years. We now have some great growth plans in place too, so hopefully in the future this will lead to the creation of more jobs – especially for young people.

We really feel that they care for us and are working in our best interests. A lot of the support we've received has been emotional and confidence building – not just financial. And Abacus supplied all this extra support at no extra cost to us, which was a wonderful gesture on their behalf.

A final word from the accountant

Paul Pritchard of Abacus added, "In order to find out how people really feel, I set up a web form and invited our clients to submit their stories through it. I was genuinely touched when I read what came back, including this one from TPPE, and I am so proud of my team for everything they have done.

"Over the years, I had got to know Mark, Anne and Maria very well, as I often assist them with the volunteer programmes they run in local schools. You will be hard pushed to find people that are more genuine and sincere than these three directors. So when Maria died it really was an emotional time for all of us. All the team at Abacus are really pleased that we've been able to help Mark and Anne through this incredibly difficult time.

"This is an unusual story as their focus has never been on the financial side of having a business – it's always been their aim to help young people make good career decisions and to give them the support and guidance they deserve.

"So what makes us most proud is that, by helping them get back on track in the face of tragedy, they are now able to make a difference to the lives of even more young people. And that is such a rewarding outcome."

Less stress, more money and more time off

Accountancy Edge is run by sole practitioner James Hellyer in Bideford, UK, and has helped a client:

- Sell a time-hungry lifestyle business for the asking price
- Develop a highly profitable second business
- Free up much more time to spend with his family

"Lots of small actions can make a huge difference to a business and the life of its owners," says James.

Background information

The client, formerly employed as a professional working in the National Health Service, had created two very different businesses in 2008:

- One provided professional services in the construction sector.

- The second provided ear protection products to surfers (surfing is a very popular activity for tourists and local people in the area).

The situation at the start

When Accountancy Edge first met the client he was running the two businesses in parallel. Both were turning over around £25,000 and both were profitable, but neither was generating anything like the income the client needed.

James explained, "The client wasn't really in touch with the numbers behind his businesses. Both were maintained on Sage Line 50 by a bookkeeper, but this was really for his accountant's benefit rather than his own. It simply made their life easier at the year-end!

"It was clear, though, that he couldn't continue to run both businesses without a great deal of stress and anxiety. Being stressed, anxious and working such long hours would mean he wasn't going to have the lifestyle he wanted with his young family."

How their accountants helped

Working closely with his client, James sought to really understand the two businesses and determine the potential of each.

"The surfer's ear protection business was more of a lifestyle option. It was ideal for someone who wanted to spend their time going to surf festivals and competitions, and selling products there to pay for the trip (and maybe a bit more). While it might be possible to grow it further, this would require even more time spent away from his home and his family."

In contrast, James ascertained that the professional services business had real opportunities for growth and increased profitability. So, after discussing and exploring the options with his client, they agreed on a strategy: sell the lifestyle business and focus 100% on making the professional services business a success.

As for the surfing business, James explains: "I provided a valuation of its trade and assets. We were then also able to identify potential purchasers, market the business to them and achieve his desired selling price."

To help his client really understand the key numbers in the remaining business, James produced much more informative, easy to understand accounting information in graphical form. He also benchmarked it against other similar businesses to identify its strengths and weaknesses. And he helped identify the key performance indicators, enabling them to target the areas of the business that needed the most focus and drive.

In addition, James migrated the bookkeeping across to a cloud based solution so they could access real time information. "This meant financial decisions were easier to make and progress on their key numbers could be measured and monitored properly."

Proactive tax planning also saved over £15,000 a year in tax, which dramatically and immediately improved the client's personal finances.

The difference it made

James explains, "The net result of this (and my client's hard work), was that the business' turnover increased from £37,000 in 2012 to £110,000 in 2015. And net profits increased from £15,000 (with no director's salary) to £75,000 (after paying a director's salary). Quite a transformation!

"He is also working fewer hours running one business, compared to when he was juggling two. And the massive increase in profitability and capital restructure has allowed him to extract significant sums from the company in the last two years to buy a rental property as his 'pension fund'. Less stress. More money. More time off. And a much brighter future. I can confidently say he is very happy with all of that!"

How it made them feel

James recalls his first meeting with his client: "At the start he was stressed and anxious because, although he was busy with both businesses, he was earning less than when he had been in full time employment, and he was working much longer hours."

"Now he is very happy with his life-work balance. He has plenty of money coming in and, just as importantly, the time to enjoy it. Which all goes to show that lots of small actions can make a huge difference to a business and the life of its owners," says James.

Helping an ambitious entrepreneur to keep her business growing

Atkinsons is a two partner firm with a team of seven, based in York, England. It has helped a client:

- Embrace cloud technology to maintain rapid growth
- Use real time financial reporting information to make better decisions and improve efficiency
- Reduce the tax bills of the business and its owner
- Buy her dream family home and dream car

"She is an exceptional entrepreneur and we're proud to have helped such a dynamic business," says the senior practitioner.

Background information

Monster Group (UK) Ltd. is an online retailer based near York, England. It supplies customers worldwide with a whole variety of products including catering equipment, weighing scales, racking systems, retail display equipment and graphic and heat press equipment.

The company was founded in 2007 by Rana Harvey and growth has been rapid from the start.

The situation at the start

Rana had taken part in the Goldman Sachs 10,000 Small Businesses Programme (which supports and develops dynamic entrepreneurs). One of the issues the programme identified was that, although the business' front end systems were dynamic and efficient, the financial reporting was lagging behind and was continually in catch-up mode. As the business continued to grow, the catch-up process was taking longer each year and although Rana had a handle on some important numbers, the Sage accounting solution they were operating no longer gave them what they needed.

Atkinsons had been recommended to Rana as a firm with a different approach to growing businesses, and they met to see if they could improve matters.

How their accountants helped

Peter Atkinson explains what they did. "First of all we identified the specific needs of Monster. Where did Rana want the business to get to? What were her personal goals? This initial review helped us formulate a plan so that we could set out a route map to help the business with its ambitious plans.

"We recommended that the business move to Xero so that their dynamic front end system could be seamlessly linked to their financial reporting, and the team could have real time information on business activity."

And the changeover process was very speedy indeed.

"One team from Atkinsons brought the Sage records up to date so that financial accounts could be quickly finalised," Peter remembers. "A second team introduced Xero within days and developed a link to the front end information. Within a week real time reports were being generated. As the live systems were put in place we also looked to develop operating plans and forecasts using our sophisticated models. Our excellent relationship with Monster's bankers helped when reviewing trade and other finance options."

Peter also spotted other opportunities to develop the business, save tax and produce positive cash savings, including:

- A review of the best way to extract funds from the business to reduce personal tax liabilities

- Introducing a new structure allowing for a tax efficient way to run company vehicles

- And most dramatic of all, a review of the freehold properties, including the warehouses owned by the business, in order to claim additional capital allowances. This has produced a significant cash refund – equivalent to five times Atkinsons' substantial annual fee. (And, as Peter explains "our fees are based on providing a total accounting solution and the savings achieved compared to employing a full time accounting employee. So those annual fees are definitely not cheap. But because they are linked to the value we provide, they represent real value for money.")

The difference it made

Monster now has access to:

- Up to date management information, with full drill down functionality, which is reviewed within days of each month end.

- Regular business performance reporting in a format required by their bank – again within days of the month end.

- Financial accounts produced within two weeks of the year end – to further support and validate the real-time information.

- Operating plans, forecasts and cash flow reports against which results can be measured.

Armed with much better management information, the business is now able to make better decisions. A key part of that process is the regular meetings that now take place with Atkinsons: monthly to consider the business's financial performance, and quarterly to review any other specific needs and identify how Atkinsons might help.

This has led to sustained growth and improved cash flow for both the business and for Rana personally.

In addition, Atkinsons has gained an excellent client – someone who acts on the advice given, has ambition backed up with flair, and who pays a substantial annual value-based fee.

"When explaining to our own team where we want our business to get to and what sort of clients we want, our shorthand is always, 'Let's get more Monsters!' Rana has referred many of her business contacts to us and the great thing is that they are entrepreneurs too – the very people we love to work with," Peter says.

How it made them feel

Rana's situation at the start was one that many business owners would envy, with rapid growth and positive cashflow. But she knew that this success would not be sustainable unless the management information issues were addressed.

Peter adds, "While we use technology widely, we never forget that it's the human contact that means our partnership with Rana and Monster can achieve great things. She now has a much better understanding of, and comfort in the reliability of, the key numbers. And that allows her to make better decisions over the future development of the business. She has very ambitious plans for the business, and we share her excitement about the possibilities for the future."

"Not only is she now feeling even more confident that she will achieve her ambitious plans. But that confidence, coupled with the even better results she is now starting to achieve and the fact that because she is now extracting cash out of the business more tax efficiently, has provided another huge benefit. It has given her the confidence, and the means, to buy her dream family home and for her husband to own the car of his dreams. So as you can imagine, her whole family are delighted."

When a client says "my accountant has changed my life" you know you are doing the right thing

A seven director practice with a team of 31 – based in Leeds, England – that has helped a client:

- Grow their £300k AV company into a £2.4m event company
- Attract blue chip customers
- Create 12 jobs
- Build a business, and leave a legacy, that he is really proud of
- Own his dream villa on a Greek island overlooking the sea
- Get the business so under control that he can spend three months a year living in his villa
- Secure long term financial security for his family and the business

As a result the client says: "I never thought I would hear myself say this... but my accountant has changed my life."

Background information

Simply Better Solutions Ltd ('SBS') is a family run business based in West Yorkshire that has always kept family values close to its heart. Originally called Project It, it was started in 2001 by Chris Holt as an audio visual ('AV') company hiring out projectors.

The situation at the start

Bartfields were appointed in 2003, when turnover was £300,000. By then SBS had already built an enviable reputation for service. But as the price of projectors fell, the market began to change, and companies started to buy their own equipment rather than hiring it in. It had therefore become clear that the business needed to change in order to be sustainable in the longer term.

That need for change was made even greater by the fact that Chris also wanted to provide long-term employment for members of his family. And he wanted to increase his disposable income in order to buy a second home abroad – and spend a lot of time living there.

How their accountants helped

Since 2003 Bartfields' lead partner David Miller has been instrumental in helping SBS rise to these challenges, re-engineer on several occasions, and exceed their business and personal goals.

The main ways they have done this have included:

- **GoalGetter** – A strategic planning day that focused on identifying the business and personal goals of Chris and his team, and the key challenges that had to be overcome in order to achieve those goals.

- **Business Edge programme** – An intensive six-month consulting programme that created a detailed improvement action plan.

- **BoardView** – Regular ongoing strategic meetings to implement, monitor and update the initial improvement action plan.

- **Ideal customer profile** – Rather than have an "anyone who comes through the door" marketing strategy, the Business Edge programme helped them to develop a clear profile of the ideal customers they would really like to work with. And then to design their entire business in order to meet the needs of those ideal customers. As a result they now target and regularly win higher quality customers, including many blue-chip businesses.

- **Business Improvement Programme** – A highly structured six-month coaching process delivered to a group of four non-competing clients. Each monthly meeting revisited key issues such as prospering through the recession, exit strategy, winning and keeping customers and getting your team on board. And each meeting resulted in a detailed action plan, for which they were held accountable at the next meeting. Chris found the process so valuable that he subsequently also put his second in command through it.

- **Grant funding** – Bartfields helped SBS identify grant funding opportunities and successfully apply for them. Some of these grants even funded the business improvement services Bartfields was supplying – making them even more affordable and valuable.

- **Costing exercise** – In order to increase profitability further, an exercise was carried out comparing the cost of acquiring new state of the art equipment against hiring in that same equipment when needed. This resulted in SBS selling the majority of their existing equipment, and instead hiring in equipment on a "when required" basis. Consequently they are now able to remain at the forefront of technology without the expense of continually updating their equipment. Which means a better service to customers with lower costs to the business.

- **Manpower review** – The costing exercise also led to a review of the business' manpower needs, resulting in several team members leaving to join the supplier which most of the old equipment was being sold to. This also freed up a significant amount of time, enabling the remaining team members to spend more time both upselling additional services and delivering world-class events.

- **Sale negotiation** – SBS's success and rapidly growing reputation resulted in a major competitor (from whom they were winning a lot of work) offering to buy them out for a substantial amount. But after protracted discussions and negotiations, Chris decided not to sell because it had become clear that he could achieve an even higher exit price, and create more of a legacy for his family, by continuing to implement the Bartfields' inspired improvement action plan.

- **Succession planning** – Initially this involved identifying the key team members needed to drive the business forward, and selling a small part of the founder's shareholding to them in order to incentivise them to make it happen. More recently it has also involved laying the foundations for them to acquire the rest of the shares via a management buyout.

- **Remuneration tax planning** – Immediately on appointment, Bartfields substantially increased the amount of money Chris was able to take home by optimising the mix of salary and dividends. And as the business has become more successful and profitable, even more advanced tax planning has further increased the percentage of pre-tax earnings the leadership team take home.

Some of the other changes this input was instrumental in bringing about included:

- **Strategic repositioning** – Rather than simply hiring out projectors (a market in decline), SBS re-engineered itself to offer a complete event organisation service.

- **Focusing on excellence** – To stand out in the event market, they made a strategic commitment to excellence in everything they do.

- **Systemising everything** – In order to make excellence a reality, they developed and continually fine-tuned world-class systems and processes for everything that matters to their customers and other stakeholders. According to David Miller, "these systems ensure that everything gets done to the same incredibly high standard, every single time. So the customers' experience is consistently outstanding."

- **Rebranding** – Given their beginnings as a projector hire company, they were originally called Project It. But with their new focus on excellence and providing a complete event organisation service, it made sense to rebrand as Simply Better Systems. As a result, their commitment to being "Simply Better" is crystal clear at all times.

- **Eliminating overreliance** – Their reputation for excellence led to them getting a large proportion of their work from a major bank. Fortunately, this overreliance on a single customer was identified before the global banking crisis and by the time it struck marketing plans had already been put in place that were attracting new ideal clients. As a result, when the bank was taken over and its new parent company switched to their existing preferred supplier, SBS was not harmed.

- **Forging strategic alliances** – Referrals play a key part in their marketing plan. But, rather than leave them to chance, the team forged strategic alliances with key hotels and other event venues in order to become their recommended supplier.

The difference it made

Bartfields' input has helped, quite literally, to transform the business from a small local AV hire company into an event organisation company with a national reputation and blue-chip customers. Their results have been transformed too:

- Their customer feedback system shows that 94% of customers rate their service as "Very good" or "Excellent"

- Turnover has grown from £300,000 to £2.4 million

- Profits are now higher than turnover used to be

- And 12 jobs have been created

And there have also been profound personal benefits for founder Chris Holt, including:

- Financial success has allowed him to achieve his personal goal of buying a plot of land on a Greek island and building a beautiful villa overlooking the sea.

- The business is no longer dependent on him – since share ownership has made his key team members fully engaged, and systemising the business has meant that others in the team can follow the systems to do (extraordinarily well) the things that previously only Chris knew how to do.

- And because the business is no longer dependent on him, he is able to spend three months a year living in his Greek villa.

- Along the way he has also been able to provide fulfilling employment for his wife, daughter and son-in-law Rob. Indeed Rob is now his second-in-command and a key part of the MBO team.

How it made them feel

In the early days life was an emotional rollercoaster: from the euphoria of winning work, to the stress of seeing the first cash flow forecasts suggesting the money would soon run out.

But Chris is now much happier: "I am no longer stressed. Why would I be? I have financial security for me and my family, a successful business, happy customers, and my dream home in the sun. What's more, the business is run brilliantly well by my team, and the management buyout we are working towards will ensure its future. So life is fantastic. Really fantastic. And to say I am proud would be an understatement.

"We definitely wouldn't have achieved all of that without the tireless help of our accountants, Bartfields. They have focused and challenged us, provided a sounding board, kept us accountable, forced us to confront the key issues, brainstormed and suggested solutions, helped us to think big, ensured we took action rather than hiding behind excuses, prevented us making mistakes, and always made sure that the numbers stacked up.

"In fact, and I never thought I would hear myself say this, but the more I think about it the more I realise it is true… my accountant has changed my life."

Preventing a family business, and the family behind it, from falling apart

BT & Co. is a 32-person practice in Topeka, USA that has helped a family business client:

- Restore trust and family relationships
- Start having fun again
- Get more buy-in from their entire team
- Create sustainable business success

"We use the story as a great case study for our team, so they can see that what we do as a firm truly matters and can change peoples' lives," says a BT & Co. director.

Background information

Logan Business Machines ('LBM') is a family owned and operated $4 million sales and service company that specialises in office equipment and document solutions. They employ 23 people and currently there are 3 generations of the Logan family working in the business.

The situation at the start

According to one of BT & Co.'s directors, Brad Koehn: "They were suffering from years of poor accounting practices, no budgets, and were handling these issues reactively. They had a motivated team, but were struggling to build and maintain good financial processes. They also lacked key systems for maintaining their inventory, getting paid, and profit margins because they did not have clarity in their numbers.

"So the leadership team was forced to spend most of their time trying to fix their accounting, and not growing their business. They were also struggling to pay their bills because they had no process for collecting their accounts receivables from customers, and did not know how to plan and forecast for the future.

51

"Consequently, it was all creating a lot of tension between the family members, the company leadership and the rest of the team. And one of the family members was on the verge of leaving the company because of the uncertainty and frustration.

"Bluntly, they were in the phase of desperation."

How their accountants helped

Brad and his team focused on:

- Working with LBM to go through their financial statements, general ledger and systems to identify, analyse and track the key data they needed.

- Facilitating a two-day strategic retreat for LBM's management team that involved a "financial mastery strategist" from BT & Co. and two business coaches from ActionCOACH. This culminated in the production of a business financial plan that includes one, three and five-year financial forecasts that are updated quarterly with progress tracking on a month-to-month basis. "The retreat and resulting plans are core to the co-coaching approach we take with our strategic partners at ActionCOACH," explains Brad.

- Giving LBM the peace of mind that comes from knowing that they have a team of experts to help them solve their challenges.

"We call ourselves 'CPAs redefined'. And part of that redefinition is that our approach is always based on the fundamental belief that one of the keys to creating sustainable success is not only to facilitate the necessary changes, but also to teach our clients what we are doing. We empower them by giving them the knowledge and know-how to keep driving their businesses forward."

The difference it made

Brad explains, "We were able to make a huge difference to our client's lives because we provided them with a team of experts to support them. The stress level of the Logan family was tremendously reduced, and they began to have fun doing what they love again.

"The leadership began to focus on how to increase sales, raise profits, improve team morale, and really concentrate on all of the things they should to grow their business. And because they now have clarity over their numbers, they are making better business decisions, which in turn are improving their profit margins and cash flow.

"We also gave them peace of mind, which allowed them to spend less time at work, but accomplish more with the time they spend at the office."

The benefits of all of this have been felt by the entire Logan team. "Their environment has shifted from tense and negative, to fun and positive. The leaders are able to spend more time with their teams and are able to communicate accurate projections, goals, and financial numbers with the entire company.

"As a result, they have gained more trust, and a greater buy-in from everyone on their team to continue to improve on a daily basis."

How it made them feel

Brad explains, "The most important thing that we were able to provide the owners was the feeling of being in control of their finances and, more importantly, their future. They began to feel the weight lifting off of their shoulders."

"We helped them:

- Overcome their fears
- Banish feelings of guilt and inadequacy, because we helped them to see that they are not the only business to struggle
- Believe that they can accomplish great things with a good team, positive attitude, and great data
- Improve their business

"And most importantly of all, we helped them to strengthen their relationships and trust as a family and as a team."

As a result, LBM became one of the firm's best referral sources. And their Vice President, Chad Logan, is on record saying, "the business community needs more companies like BT & Co., that honestly, accurately, and excitedly help local businesses proactively grow their finances, culture, and market share."

The firm also uses the story of how they have helped LBM "as a great case study for our team, so they can see that what we do as a firm truly matters and can change peoples' lives."

"Even more important than stemming the losses was restoring a sense of pride"

A two partner practice with a team of 17 based in Kent, UK.
The practice has made a radical difference to their client.

- Reversed losses of £50,000 per month – and has never made a loss since
- 23 jobs saved and 14 more created
- The business owner's sense of pride restored
- Family business of 50 years standing saved from failure

Partner Nick Hume says, "We sometimes rather glibly say that our work can change lives, however we usually mean financially. On this occasion I realised the huge non-financial value of what an accountant can achieve."

Background information

The business is owned by Fred (name changed to preserve confidentiality), with turnover of £2.5 million and was started in the 1960s by his father. Fred is personally wealthy with a large house in the countryside, a Ferrari and a holiday home in Spain.

The situation at the start

Calcutt Matthews was approached about the business by Barclays Bank in 2011. The practice had previously made the bank aware that they liked to help resuscitate businesses that were struggling, but weren't at the stage of requiring a receiver or liquidation.

The business had been losing £50,000 per month for some time. It was overstaffed and orders had fallen to the point that the business owner had taken to using some of the staff who weren't busy to refurbish his own house. One of the divisions was a disaster, with highly unpredictable sales, very little work billed and low profitability on the work that was billed. The pricing structure for the main business was also poorly thought out.

The bank manager was concerned that the bank was exposed to approximately £500,000 worth of debt and had insufficient security.

How their accountants helped

At the initial meeting Nick sat down with the business owner and for two hours he just listened. "That's what Fred seemed to need at that moment; someone who wasn't involved who would really listen to him. What came out of that was how terrible he felt that the company his father had started 50 years ago was in jeopardy.

"At the end I asked Fred what he wanted to achieve. He simply said that he wanted to make his family proud and save the business. I was certain we could help."

Nick then used AVN's Business Potential software to generate ideas for business growth (the software identifies small changes that can be made in a business to make it more profitable). He first created a model for wiping out the losses and then another that would allow the company to make £50,000 per month.

The software directed attention to improving margins and an examination of why orders had fallen.

The company had an excellent website that was attracting a lot of attention. But when potential customers contacted them the process fell apart. The estimator who handled new queries either under-priced, failed to get back to the customers quickly or caused confusion in his communication. It was clear that he either needed to be trained or let go. At the business owner's request he was quickly replaced. However, the key element in halting the cash haemorrhage arose from the bold decision to close down the division that was in the biggest mess.

The difference it made

Incredibly, with Nick's help, the business had stopped making losses by the end of the first month of Calcutt Matthews' involvement.

In addition:

- After nine weeks the business made its first £50,000 profit
- 23 jobs were saved

- A further 14 jobs have been created
- Fred's son has also now started working in the business after graduating from university

"Apart from a short December (seasonally affected by an early closing for Christmas) the business then went on to make at least £50,000 every month for the six months that followed. Since that date the company has never made a loss in any month as result of our working very closely with the owner and his co-directors."

While Fred has increased his spend with Calcutt Matthews by 50% per year, for Nick the level of trust between them is the most important result of working together and he is keen to do even more for the client.

How it made them feel

At the start, Fred was hugely embarrassed that the business his father started and that had been in the family for 50 years could be lost. He couldn't bear to face his father and tell him how bad things were.

"I went to meet Fred after nine weeks of working with us," Nick comments. "The company had just made its first £50,000 profit and we believed it could sustain this profitability.

"I mentioned to Fred that I would like to take him out to lunch to celebrate. As an average height, fairly reserved English accountant I thought this the most appropriate way of celebrating success. However, Fred, who stands six foot five and is about double my weight, said just one thing –'Nick, can I have a hug?'

"Well, I have to admit I was thrown a little, but I obliged of course!

"Driving away later I realised I had been focusing on re-establishing cash in the bank and desperately trying to save the business. I had completely missed the point that far more important to this client was what he would say to his father, his wife, his son and daughter. The most important thing for him was not just stemming the losses, but restoring a sense of pride.

"Wonderful though it is to save our clients a lot of tax or help them grow their profits by an extra 20%, nothing is more worthwhile than restoring that pride and saving the jobs of their workers."

Helping to build a bright future for a married couple

Chris Beks of Ceebeks Business Solutions is a sole practitioner with a team of three based in Warrnambool, Victoria, Australia who has helped a client:

- Take advantage of a once in a lifetime opportunity to buy their own business
- Exceed forecasts in repayment of debts
- Build a dated motel into a thriving part of the community

"We're so proud of being able to help this client achieve their dream," Chris says.

Background information

Raj and Bronwyn Patel have run the Best Western Olde Maritime Motor Inn in Warrnambool since 2014.

The situation at the start

Raj and Bronwyn are long standing clients of Chris Beks at Ceebeks Business Solutions; in fact, Chris helped Raj to migrate to Australia more than 20 years ago, after the couple met in the UK and fell in love. So when he was offered the opportunity of a lifetime to buy his own business he and Bronwyn turned to Chris for help.

Raj had been working in the motel industry in Warrnambool ever since he arrived in Australia. He had built up an outstanding reputation as a motel manager and in 2014 was offered the franchise of the local Best Western motel, where he had been employed for over 10 years. Owning their own business had been the couple's dream for a long time and this was the chance for them to actually make it happen. However, they had modest savings and no access to the capital they would need to buy the leasehold.

How their accountants helped

"Because of the longstanding relationship we have with Raj and Bronwyn we knew and understood them really well, especially their financial position," Chris explains.

"Even though there were significant problems due to the lack of savings and asset backing, I was sure they had a chance of getting the finance they needed. Raj's reputation and his rapport with both guests and suppliers meant there was a lot of goodwill towards him from the vendor and I felt that with a robust business plan we could be successful."

So Chris prepared a case he could take to the bank. As part of this he:

- Created a detailed business plan with a five year budgeted balance sheet, profit and loss and cash flow projections.

- Outlined the key objectives for borrowing a significant sum, using the Patel's home as security.

- Set out the time frame for reducing the debt and developed a detailed plan to improve occupancy rates through refurbishment and upgrades to the building.

The difference it made

The bank agreed to provide both a loan and an overdraft facility, and the vendor also helped to finalise the deal for Raj and Bronwyn.

Chris helped to implement a Xero accounting system to give Raj instantly accessible data. He also set up monthly meetings, at which they monitor results against the budget forecasts, tweak occupancy and rack rates and plan staffing levels.

As a result, in the first 12 months of operations:

- Bank debt was reduced by 22% (comfortably exceeding forecasts)
- Vendor debt was reduced by 33%
- Occupancy rates have increased by 5%
- All rooms have been refurbished
- The motel restaurant has become a local favourite!

How it made them feel

Chris's motto for his practice is 'the lifestyle accountants who impact lives', and that's exactly what he's done for Raj and Bronwyn.

Having seen the potential to change the business from a dated, old fashioned motel to a vibrant asset to the town, they were anxious and scared that they might not be able to make it happen. And even once the bank loan had been secured they were worried about putting their family at risk through taking on a large amount of debt.

But after the first 12 months they were thrilled with the success of the business – and were even able to celebrate with a luxurious family holiday in Thailand.

"We are so grateful for the outstanding service that Chris and his team have provided. Right from the start their advice and assistance has been absolutely invaluable. Ceebeks Business Solutions is now an integral part of our operation and we simply wouldn't be in business without them."

"It's like going to work in a totally different business."

A sole practitioner with a small team from Nottingham, England who helped a client:

- Extract themselves from an unhappy and hostile business relationship
- Increase sales year on year by 19.8%
- Give their employees a pay rise for the first time in five years
- Clear a £42,500 overdraft in just six months

The client comments, "The change between where we were then and where we are now is just phenomenal."

Background information

Glazedale Ltd. manufactures and installs high quality, bespoke double glazing and has a number of 'grand design' projects under its belt.

The company was started in 1988 by Darren Shelbourn and became a division of K & A Cox Ltd. in 1999, a merger which was intended to capitalise on synergies between Glazedale's double glazing and K & A Cox's focus on curtains and blinds. K & A Cox Ltd. had started in 1949 and was a typical family-run business.

The shareholding of the company was split equally between the four shareholders: Darren and his wife Claudia, and the two shareholders originally with K & A Cox.

The situation at the start

When Claudia joined the business as a director in 2006 she began to see problems that had previously been hidden:

- There were no management accounts and nobody was properly controlling the finances.

- The husband and wife directors from the K & A Cox division were resistant to making any changes and had a 'we've always done it this way' attitude.

- There was a growing sense of unfairness that the Glazedale side of the business was propping up K & A Cox, but financial information was so poor it was impossible to be certain of the true situation.

- The shareholders were unable to agree on the need for strategic financial planning and day-to-day cashflow management and there were personality clashes between the two sides.

The company was facing financial strains and as the economic climate worsened, the future of the business looked bleak.

How their accountants helped

Before Coalesco came on board, the company used a firm of accountants who provided a purely compliance service, taking an annual fee and offering no business improvement support.

When this firm began to offer a business consultancy service and charge for advice that essentially amounted to 'sell more', the directors decided that they needed more substantive proactive support from their accountant. This became even more urgent when they discovered that the shareholders had been inadvertently withdrawing illegal dividends due to the lack of good quality data.

After interviewing three new firms of accountants and some heated discussions amongst the shareholders, they appointed Linda Frier from Coalesco.

Linda remembers, "Our first task together was a practical one – to establish just how poor the Sage data and processes were. We ran one first year end which was quite a task because of incorrect historical balances and no reconciliations. The results were weaker than expected so, due to a reluctance to change software, we installed an upgrade to Sage so we could get the divisional reporting the company needed."

Straight away, it became obvious that K &A Cox was making significant losses and not even contributing towards overheads. Linda adds, "It was no wonder that resentment had been building given that the split between the two pairs of shareholders was 50/50."

By February 2013, Linda had developed proper management accounting and introduced Key Performance Indicators. She could see that the business simply wouldn't survive if it continued to run as it had been, but once again, the attitude of 'we've always done it this way' blocked progress.

By September, relations between the two pairs of shareholders were becoming increasingly difficult and Darren was at a very low point. This was when Linda first suggested demerging the two businesses. Initially, Darren and Claudia felt it would be financially impossible, but Linda persevered. "At Christmas time," she remembers, "I told them that this time next year they'd be in two separate places with the business."

They then had a stroke of good luck when the other shareholders themselves suggested a demerger. This was the opportunity Linda had been waiting for. "I facilitated an agreement between the four of them," she says. "Claudia and Darren would retain the building and the company's trading history; K & A Cox would commence as a separate legal entity and have space within the building as a tenant; and they would each keep their own stock on hand at the demerger date."

Remarkably, with Coalesco's support, it took just three months to complete the entire process, including banking, building works, vehicle transfers and supplier and customer communications.

Specifically, Coalesco:

- Helped Darren and Claudia to find the £100,000 of funding they needed to buy out the other shareholders.

- Trained Claudia to fully understand every aspect of the company's finances and implemented systems, controls and processes including full month end shut down.

- Changed the accounting software to Xero for better data collaboration and improved management reporting and gave Claudia full training on how to use it.

- Invited Claudia to their quarterly educational seminars to give her a solid grounding to take on significant responsibilities.

The difference it made

- A £42,500 overdraft was cleared in the space of six months.
- Loyal employees have had a pay rise for the first time in five years.

- With a clear cashflow forecast in place Darren and Claudia no longer have to fund the business personally as had happened many times previously.

- Sales are up year on year by 19.8%, gross margin has increased from 28% to 32.6% and overheads reduced by £14,000.

- Their fleet of vehicles has been upgraded, improving the brand image and increasing employee motivation as well as lowering maintenance costs.

- Dedicated showroom space has allowed Glazedale to develop their product offering and renew their enthusiasm to make more profit.

- The company was able to support BBC television's DIY SOS programme and help a local family in urgent need of help to make their home suitable for a disabled family member. They would never have been able to do this previously.

- They now have 22 employees and an average turnover of £140,000 per month.

With Linda's careful facilitation, the two pairs of directors parted ways amicably, something that would have surprised them all a few months previously.

How it made them feel

At the start, Darren and Claudia were feeling disheartened by the obstructive attitude they faced daily from their fellow directors, frustrated by their lack of ability to influence change and demoralised by an intense sense of unfairness.

Now, decisions can be made quickly and easily. Claudia says, "It's such a relief not to be beholden to anyone other than Darren and the bank manager! Darren is a different person to work with and it feels like it's worth going to work now that we can see the fruits of our own efforts and reward staff in the ways they should be."

They are optimistic, enjoying having a common goal for the future, in control and able to make the choices that matter to them. This whole period has proved life changing in every way.

Turning losses into profits by focusing on the low hanging fruit

EBCFO is a four person practice in Missouri, USA that has helped a client:

- Transform unreliable estimates into robust data
- Identify the source of their losses
- Add $160,000 to their bottom line

"It has rekindled all of the exciting feelings they had when they set out in business, and they are able to dream big again," says the firm's founder.

Background information

EBCFO's client is a commercial construction company.

The situation at the start

Despite being exceptionally good at what it does, the business was making losses that amounted to 10% of their total sales. As EBCFO's founder Dan Schmidt explains, "Their job estimates for each piece of work always suggested they were making profits. But their antiquated desktop accounting system showed that the business as a whole was making losses, without giving them any useful insights as to why."

How their accountants helped

"The first thing we needed to do was to help them understand that they were placing far too much reliance on unsupported accounting and profitability estimates," says Dan. "We explained that they needed to base their decisions on far more reliable, robust and accurate real-time information. And we set them up with cloud accounting software that had been designed specifically for the construction industry to give them the decision support insights they desperately wanted and needed."

Finally armed with reliable data, EBCFO were able to benchmark the business against others in similar areas of the construction industry. This in turn helped them to:

- Identify that labour costs (at 82% of sales) were far higher than industry norms – and help the owners focus on improving productivity and efficiency to bring the labour cost percentage down.

- Realise that they were also spending far more on small tools than others in their industry – which on further investigation turned out to be because whenever the on-site workers needed a tool they sent a runner to the nearest shop to buy a new one, rather than on the slightly longer journey to simply borrow one from the business' tool store!

- Persuade the client to reduce the number of jobs they quoted for. "In the past they quoted for everything. Not only did this cost them a lot of time and money, but very often it resulted in them winning jobs that they weren't well suited to do, and couldn't therefore make a good profit on."

"We aren't stopping there, though," explains Dan. "So far we haven't been able to move them on to Xero because it didn't fully support the construction industry. But very soon it will, so we will be switching them to that in order to tap into the extra insights, power and functionality of apps such as the management information dashboards that Crunchboards creates at the push of a button."

The difference it made

Since they started working with EBCFO 12 months ago the client has already seen a $160,000 improvement in its profitability – moving from 10% losses to 6% profits. And that stabilisation of their previously precarious position has allowed them to stay in business, and look forward to a much more successful future.

"Because there are so many issues that businesses face, and so many potential ways of tackling them, they often have no idea where to start. So we believe that a key part of our role is always to help them to focus on and prioritise the quick wins, low hanging fruit, and the things they are really good at. That way they will get the best return on their investment of time and effort. It's exactly what we did with this client, and the results prove that it is an approach that works."

How it made them feel

"When we started working with them they were optimistic, but confused. They had no idea why things were going wrong. And they have felt like hamsters in a wheel – running round and round without actually getting anywhere.

"Now, just 12 months later, they feel like they've been set free from that wheel. It has rekindled all of the exciting feelings they had when they set out in business, and they are able to dream big again, doing what they love to do."

Helping clients in these sorts of ways is also working out very well for Dan. Until recently the practice was just a hobby sideline for him. But in the 18 months since it became a full-time business it has grown from 5 to 100 clients, using cloud technology to support dynamic businesses in seven US states.

"Despite all that growth, I am still able to leave the office no later than 5 PM every single day to spend precious time with my three young children. That is really important to me. So I'm delighted too," says Dan.

Rescued from bankruptcy as a result of wiping out tax liabilities

Galbraith Rushby is a two partner firm, with approximately 40 staff in Woodstock, South Africa that has helped a client to:

- Prevent the taxman taking 5 million South African Rand
- Avoid personal bankruptcy
- Keep their family homes

"They were unbelievably relieved," says one of the founders.

The story below is an "in her own words" account by one of Galbraith Rushby's founders, Jeneen Galbraith.

Background information

"The client is a professional services group, who had employed over 30 people. Despite many years of success it lost a major government contract and hit very hard times.

The situation at the start

As a result of the loss of the government contract, the business quickly spiralled downwards due to the high rental charges, salaries and other overheads. As the position worsened and their cash flow was used to cover the overhead costs, they fell behind in making their SARS (the South African Revenue Service tax authority) payments. As soon as a payment is late to SARS it incurs a 10% penalty and interest is added to the debt. The figures quickly climbed to an amount of R3.8m. SARS and other creditors began "calling" for their money.

As soon as we saw the financial position, we advised that they cut back on permanent staff, keep a core pool of staff that they could call on as independent contractors when required and scale down to smaller premises. The client however, kept believing that they would be awarded another contract and be able to recover from their position. In addition, they changed accountants to another firm, who told them they had connections within SARS and who could assist in getting rid of their SARS debt.

However, when they came back to us things had got even worse. They still owed a bigger debt to SARS and they were further behind in their tax affairs than before. They were facing personal bankruptcy and for one of the partners, this meant losing his family home, which would have resulted in the break down and possible loss of relationship with his family.

Whilst business was crumbling around him, he was holding onto his family and his greatest fear was to lose them as well.

How their accountants helped

The first thing we did was to engage with SARS, explain what had happened and offer a settlement figure of a percentage of the debt. Since they still owned property, they largely funded this settlement figure by selling a property. There was still quite a process to go through and future tax compliance was an important part of the agreement.

From bad to worse

Just when we thought that they were in the clear, with business overheads reduced, a small handful of staff, more modest premises, the SARS debts paid and the prospect of future work coming in, SARS decided to do a VAT audit on previous financial periods.

Whilst doing this audit, SARS said that they should have paid VAT on the properties which they had sold instead of transfer duty. This amounted to a figure of R1.2 million. This is what I call a "double jeopardy tax situation". They had sold the properties to pay outstanding SARS debt and now they were required to pay further money despite the fact that they had paid the sale proceeds over to SARS.

SARS argued that since these properties were owned by a VAT registered entity and were used by their business they were subject to VAT whereas normally residential properties are exempt from VAT and only subject to transfer duty.

We prepared a very thorough and detailed technical counter argument and we were able to show that despite the fact that the business had housed employees this did not change the nature of the residence from residential to commercial and thus VAT was not applicable.

The difference it made and how it made them feel

When SARS accepted our objection and reversed the VAT, the client was ecstatic and couldn't believe it. They had been so used to bad news and being in financial trouble. This allowed them to have a fresh start.

Throughout this whole process, we were working very hard and time was clocking up on their account. A worrying factor for us was that they, of course, could not pay these fees which had now amounted to 300,000 Rand.

Since our philosophy is to be there for our clients in good times and in bad, we discussed with them they would pay off the amount slowly over the next few years but that they should keep current with all new bills. This was an arrangement that they gladly accepted and we know that they will be our clients for life.

Our philosophy of personal service and attention at reasonable rates has been one of our key success factors and has led to the growth of our firm over the past 8 years from one staff member to our current levels of over 40 staff."

"We wouldn't even have started the business if it wasn't for our accountant"

Growthwise is a four partner practice with seven team members, based in Newcastle, Australia that has helped a client:

- Start up a business that had previously just been a dream
- Put systems and tools in place to enable sustainable growth right from the start
- Grow a business from zero to five offices in just four years

"Without Growthwise our business would never have got off the ground," the clients say.

Background information

MCG Quantity Surveyors specialise in construction cost estimating and tax depreciation schedules for residential and commercial property investors. Based in Newcastle, New South Wales, they service mainly New South Wales, Queensland and Victoria.

The situation at the start

MCG started in 2011 with no clients, no systems and no processes. The owners knew they wanted their own business and they were good at what they did, but they had no idea of where to start or what to do.

They approached Steph Hinds of Growthwise to ask for help. "They felt paralysed," she says now. "They had so many questions about running their own business and none of the answers."

In fact, they had been thinking about starting up on their own for three years, but it was only when they talked to Steph that they realised they could actually make their dream a reality.

How their accountants helped

Steph had developed a programme specifically for this situation. Called 'L Platers', it covers everything new business owners need to know over a 12 month programme. As the Growthwise website puts it - 'Think, Learn, Grow & Kick Arse'!

So Steph started the owners on the programme. "We made them plan and focus each month on a different part of the business, understanding in detail what the numbers mean when growing quickly; how, who and when to employ; and implementing technology to ensure the admin side of things didn't take over the business.

"We implemented Xero, Debtor Daddy (debtor tracking software) and Workflow Max (job management software) and ensured they had tools like eWAY (a payment platform) set up so that anything they needed to know was just one click away and nothing needed to be entered into multiple systems. Our big focus was setting up systems for them that were simple – #banadmin! We didn't want to be paying unnecessary admin wages that would just increase with volume."

The L-Platers programme is designed to help business owners stay motivated, continuously focus on improvement and challenge themselves to keep growing, all while maintaining sustainable cashflow.

The difference it made

More than anything, Steph's help meant that MCG moved from an idea to an actual business. And that they started off with the right systems and tools in place, and an action plan that was continuously reviewed and updated.

"They are running the business with great growth, but also great profitability. They are thinking and planning ahead for years of growth to come. They are utilising the technology solutions we have implemented to ensure they don't have to employ administrators to type in data (which results in higher profits). And they have all the information at the click of a few buttons to enable them to make informed decisions."

As MCG grows, five new jobs have been created and they have been able to serve thousands of clients and in turn, save them thousands of dollars in tax.

Steph adds, "Our client wants to keep their exact financials confidential, but it's fair to say that they are enjoying tremendous success, with sales growing at 200% a year and profits ramping up every year too. So they are definitely kicking arse!"

The relationship between MCG and Growthwise has strengthened over the years and Growthwise is now the first place the owners turn to for help. As the business has developed, MCG has moved from the L Platers programme to 'Black Ops', the Growthwise business advice programme.

"We become a partner to keep the business owner laser focused and on track," Steph explains. "We put the spotlight on action and ensure the owner is accountable for achieving their goals and we work together to develop a strategy and practical action plan, monitor progress, be a sounding board and most importantly educate business owners on how to kick-arse!"

How it made them feel

The business owners have this to say about Growthwise – "In terms of performance, Growthwise is like a Duracell enema. They're always bursting with enthusiasm and I always leave their office brimming with confidence to smash our business goals."

Uncovering serious errors helped protect the client's reputation

Hunter Gee Holroyd is a three director accountancy firm with a team of 30, based in Yorkshire, England. The firm has helped a client to:

- Uncover and correct serious mistakes made by the previous accountant
- Obtain a significant Corporation Tax repayment
- Avoid making redundancies during the years of the recession
- Build a strong and trusting relationship that furthers the aims of the business

"They understand our business and they genuinely care about what happens to it," says the client.

Background information

Burn & Company is a well-established legal firm based in the outskirts of the city of York, with 30 employees and annual turnover of around £1 million. It is one of the founding members of the Quality Solicitors brand, a nationwide network of law firms. Previously a partnership, they became a limited company in 2009.

The situation at the start

When the partners made the decision to change the business to a limited company, they knew that their accounts would be made public at Companies House. With a strong reputation to protect they needed to be certain that everything was in perfect order before the change could go ahead. However, their existing accountant was not delivering a level of service that gave them any confidence and as the transition continued they became increasingly unhappy.

73

How their accountants helped

Mark Burn, formerly a partner and now a director of the business, had been attending regular Business Builder Forum business seminars at Hunter Gee Holroyd (HGH) for several years. The seminars are designed to help business owners become more successful through exposure to new ideas and best practice and support from their peers. Mark had built up a strong relationship with two of HGH's directors, Nigel Atkinson and Mark Grewer.

When it came to finding a new accountant for Burn & Company, HGH were top of the list as they had already shown Mark how proactive they were on behalf of their clients. They were appointed in June 2011.

When HGH prepared the accounts for the year ended 31st October 2011, it became apparent to them that several significant errors had been made within the previous year's accounts and in the associated Corporation Tax computations and Return form (all created by the previous accountant). The most significant errors were an incorrect treatment of work in progress and an incorrect calculation on the capital allowance claim.

Other small errors meant that the taxable profit was overstated by the previous accountant by £282,021 and the Corporation Tax liability by £61,727.

HGH contacted HMRC and submitted amended Corporation Tax computations. After much correspondence and communication, HMRC issued a tax repayment of £61,727 to the business, but two months later opened an enquiry into the amended Corporation Tax Return form.

The enquiry into the Return covered not just the areas which had been discovered, but also a more detailed analysis of various items in the profit and loss account. This led to protracted correspondence with HMRC, Burn & Company and the previous accountant to obtain information to respond to the various queries.

The work involved a detailed review of the nominal ledgers and treatment of expenditure by the previous accountant. Correspondence with HMRC continued over eight stressful months but eventually led to various adjustments, some in favour of HMRC and others in favour of Burn & Company. The reduction in the tax repayment came to just £957.

However, the revised capital allowance claim initially made and increased due to the bulk of the adjustments amounted to £15,919, with the carry forward balance increased by £36,016 (saving £7,203 in tax in future years).

The difference it made

While HGH was diligent and persistent in dealing with the HMRC enquiry, the real difference lies in the trusting and personal relationship they have built up with Mark.

- HGH proactively discusses and advises on accounts and business development so Mark and his fellow directors understand what is happening in their business.

- During the recession when there was a reduction of work, HGH liaised with the bank to keep them informed of cashflow balances and issues with clients extending payment deadlines. They helped to ensure the liquidity of the business and avoid making redundancies.

- The unexpected repayment of Corporation Tax early into the relationship greatly assisted the cashflow of the business.

How it made them feel

"Delighted and relieved," is how Mark Burn describes his feelings about working with HGH. "When our previous accountant caused so much stress and worry, it's a massive relief to know that everything is being handled absolutely professionally. HGH have really taken the time to understand our business and they give us the information we need to drive it forwards in the way we want."

Using cloud technology to keep investors happy and prevent further dilution of ownership

Inform Accounting is a one director, nine person firm in Sutton Coldfield, England that has helped a client to:

- Harness the power of cloud technology
- Prevent stock issues becoming a major drain on cashflow
- Give their investors the information and comfort they need
- Avoid diluting their ownership

"I am about to receive share options as a thank you," says Inform Accounting's director.

Background information

Learning Labs was founded by Veejay Lingiah and Richard Allen to produce FlashSticks: foreign language Post-it® Notes, each printed with a unique, commonly used word, translation, icon, and gender colour-coding. Their supporting app allows customers to hover their tablet or smartphone over any FlashStick, in order to get a pop up tutor revealing exactly how to pronounce the word you're struggling with.

It is an early stage company, established approximately 3 years ago, that has outside investors and is growing steadily as it gains orders from major blue chip retailers.

The situation at the start

"Despite being a young company, when we started working with them 18 months ago they were using legacy accounting systems. They had a bookkeeper using Sage and a part time Finance Director producing stock and cashflow forecasts in Sage Winforecast for the investor board meetings," says Inform Accounting's director Sian Kelly.

"It was all based on out of date historic numbers, with no flexibility to run different scenarios. So it was causing considerable frustration amongst the investors at a time when the management really needed to be on top of their financial information to maintain investor confidence and ensure a second round of funding could be achieved."

How their accountants helped

Sian summarises the help they provided as follows:

- **Cloud accounting** – "We immediately switched them onto Xero (using MoveMyBooks to automate transferring the data across) so that we had real time up to date financial information for the board meetings, and used Receipt Bank for collecting and processing purchase invoices and expenses. Together these changes meant that any queries arising could be answered immediately."

- **Cloud reporting** – "We set them up with Spotlight Reporting to produce the monthly board pack and management accounts in an impressive, understandable and insightful format."

- **Cloud stock management** – "Unleashed was implemented as their stock system in December 2014, and off the back of this a full forecasting model for stock, P&L, balance sheet and cashflow has been built, all driven off expected product demand, from a starting point of current stock levels. This was particularly valuable as there is a 10 week lead time for production and delivery to the UK, so without reliable information they would either have kept running out of stock or had to overcompensate by holding really high, and really costly, stock levels."

- **Cloud cashflow management** – "We also introduced them to Market Invoice, which claims to be the largest online invoice finance platform in the world, and which certainly helped them to fund their growth by raising cash easily, quickly and selectively against their outstanding sales invoices at the push of a button from inside their accounting system."

The difference it made

As a result, the business is now able to:

- Understand and plan for cashflow constraints, rather than having to go cap in hand to investors at the last minute

- Plan stock levels accurately, preventing costly over ordering and reducing the funds tied up in stock, and

- Keep its investors happy by giving them the information, reassurance, cash flow stability and evidence of success that they are looking for.

Crucially, by being able to properly manage their cash flow and use tools such as Market Invoice to bridge finance gaps, the founders have been able to hold off on further funding rounds. So they have prevented further dilution, and kept ownership of a larger stake in the business.

How it made them feel

Sian explains, "When we started working with them they felt very vulnerable because they were working with out of date information. But now they are very confident that they understand what is going on, have reliable forecasts, and are able to present 'worst case' scenarios to the board when needed.

"It's been a very rewarding relationship for us too, as we are already working with several people they have introduced us to, and I am about to receive share options as a thank you for reducing our fees to support their cash flow.

"I believe the profession is at a crossroads," adds Sian. "Some accountants are helping customers integrate and automate things, improving accuracy and reliability, saving time and reducing costs. And others seem to be happy to allow their clients to limp along with legacy technology and systems that are slow, inefficient, costly and error prone. The first group are enabling economic progress, growth and prosperity. And not only are we proud to be part of it, but for the good of the profession we urge other accountants to join it too."

Living up to their name as inspiring and innovative accountants

Inspire CA is a two partner, 11 person firm in Newstead, Australia, that has:

- Helped a client grow to $1.6 million in sales and create 20 new jobs
- Changed the lives of 90,191 people in need
- Built itself around a uniquely innovative Inspire Cafe

"As well as a great client, I have also gained a great friend who shares my passion for making a difference," says their Chief Inspiration Officer, Ben Walker.

Background information

MyCladders is a Brisbane based metal roofing and metal cladding company, founded in 2004 by Kendrick Myers.

The situation at the start

Inspire CA's founder, Ben Walker, explains, "They came to us looking for some help growing their business. At the time they were effectively a labour hire business. They were only contracting to one customer, and were only supplying hours of labour (no materials). The hours and workload were dictated by the contractor (i.e. middleman) and so business growth was limited and out of their control."

How their accountants helped

Kendrick already knew that the answer was to get a licence so that he could contract directly with builders in the retail market, without needing a middleman. But he hadn't done it because he felt he needed more accountability and confidence to move ahead.

In a video on Inspire CA's website he says, "I wanted more, but didn't have any confidence. Inspire has given our whole business the tools and the confidence to go out there and get things done. They've said you need to get this, then this, and then this done. Once you get that done, you can move to another step. And thanks to them we have now done all of that, and two steps more!"

As for accountability, explains Ben, "We set them up with a suite of integrated Xero-based cloud accounting and management systems. So they now have a much better insight into the key numbers, and much more control over the entire business. It also gives them far more team engagement, and greatly improved efficiency, as their team can simply login to do their timesheets, apply for leave and holidays, and even report sickness. And it allows us to work closely alongside them to monitor everything in real time, and continually suggest ways to make things better."

The difference it made

Since they started working with their new accountants, MyCladders:

- Has grown from $670,000 to $1.6 million in sales

- Are now quoting for $300,000-$500,000 of work each week, and has also

- Created 20 new jobs – with the original team of two now growing to 5 full time and 17 part time employees

How it made them feel

According to Ben, the best aspect of all this success was summed up when Kendrick said, "We support 5 families through 5 full time jobs. And they all have children. So for us to be able to support those families, gives us more drive and a lot of happiness. Because that's what we're here for: not just to grow ourselves, but to grow others around us too."

As for Ben himself, "As well as a great client, I have also gained a great friend in Kendrick who shares my passion for making a difference. So much so, in fact, that I asked him to be a groomsman at my wedding recently. And I'm really proud to say that he was there by my side on my big day."

But the inspiration doesn't end there

Inspire CA lives up to its name in many other ways. For example:

- Publishing a monthly newsletter, "Inspiring business"

- Giving away free copies of its book, "5 numbers all business owners need to know"

- Being a "B1G1: Business For Good", and changing the lives of people in need across the world by making 90,191 micro-givings through www.B1G1.com – at least one micro-giving for every email it sends, meeting it holds, AGM it attends, strategic planning session it runs and coffee and meal it sells in the Inspire Café.

The state-of-the-art and purpose-built Inspire Cafe, which the entire business is centred around, is perhaps its most extraordinarily creative initiative. Decked in stunning bright red cladding (supplied by MyCladders) it offers the normal range of up-market cafe services. But, uniquely, it is also a business hub, meeting room, seminar venue and executive lounge.

During our 17 years of research, we have never seen anything like the Inspire Cafe anywhere else in the world. It has to be seen to be believed – and you can see it at www.inspireca.com.

Given all of this innovation, it is no wonder that Ben's job title is Chief Inspiration Officer or that the firm's website says the following:

"Ben started Inspire CA to head in the opposite direction to the traditional 'old way' of the accounting industry. Forget time sheets; forget charging by the hour; forget difficult to use software and glazing over in conversations with your accountant. Inspire CA is for the business owner who wants to understand what drives their business, while partnering with an accounting firm who takes care of the rest."

"My accountant opened my eyes to the potential within my business"

A sole practitioner based in Birmingham, England, who has helped a client:

- Obtain £165,000 in funding to aid business growth
- Build a business that runs without him being there
- Create 9 jobs with a further 4 in the pipeline
- Become the 'go to' organisation in their sector
- Understand the huge potential of the business

As the client says, "They showed me how much value there was in my business and how I could be much more profitable."

Background information

Trade Management Services Limited (TMS) is a support organisation for the events and catering sector, focusing on mobile caterers and street food sellers. Founded by Bob Fox in 2005, the company is based in the Kings Norton area of Birmingham.

TMS provides support and training in the areas of hygiene, health and safety, legal support and insurance, delivered via web based training and courses, membership packs and insurance cover. They also help their members find new opportunities at upcoming events.

The situation at the start

The cost of TMS membership was low, as Bob felt that his client base had limited resources and that he could offer only a narrow range of benefits.

He was also anxious to avoid a repeat of a previous business experience, when, in a similar organisation, the insurers who were providing cover to its members pulled out of the deal. They started offering insurance services direct to the members, bypassing the company that Bob was operating.

On that occasion he formed TMS from the remains of the previous company and managed to win back some former members, but was understandably keen to keep costs to a minimum. Converting his garage into an office, he ran the business from there with the help of his son, Alan.

How their accountants helped

Although he had been a client of James, Stanley & Co. for several years, it was only when Bob attended one of their seminars in 2009 that he understood that his business could achieve a lot more.

The seminar, called *Pricing for maximum profit*, helped Bob realise that TMS was offering its members something of huge value that warranted a membership price far greater than what they were currently being charged. The key value points for members were:

- Peace of mind in knowing that they had fully complied with legislation
- City & Guilds accreditation through the TMS online training
- Insurance cover
- Access to TMS' extensive knowledge of the catering sector

There was clearly great potential in the business, but they needed help to make it a reality.

Andrew James, who had delivered the seminar, discussed pricing with Bob and persuaded him to raise his prices. And Bob was genuinely surprised that when he properly explained the benefits of membership, the increases met with little resistance.

Andrew and Bob also discussed bundling, and came up with a series of different bundles of services and support to offer to members. Bob further developed the TMS training courses and in many cases he was able to increase the services that members bought.

Membership renewals were another challenge. At the anniversary date of a membership the team at TMS had to call them, ask if they were going to renew and then take payment. Andrew therefore suggested trying out direct debits instead and this has helped enormously:

- Renewals are now less fuss and less work

- They can now offer a staged payment arrangement to those who cannot afford the increased membership fees in one payment. This minimised any reduction in membership due to the price increase.

As the company grew it became clear that they needed more than just annual accounts in order to get to grips with the trading performance. In 2012 James, Stanley & Co. started preparing quarterly management accounts for the company and began attending their quarterly board meetings at which the financials are discussed and the plans are set for the next period.

With this additional input, Andrew was able to help with two new initiatives:

- Expansion of online training for businesses and individuals who are not members of TMS. Andrew and the team helped with the tax planning for this new venture and set up a new business, NCASS Enterprises LLP, to operate it. All of the directors' cars (four in total) are run very tax efficiently through this Limited Liability Partnership.

- TMS applied for and was awarded a grant of £100,000 from the Birmingham Post Growth Fund. Team members from James, Stanley & Co. assisted in the application process and put together the first claim under the grant. This funding will enable TMS to recruit four additional team members to handle marketing and another recent new venture into catering product sales. (STOP PRESS: A further £65,000 in grant finding has also now been obtained).

With this grant, TMS is now properly funded to continue on its expansion path and able to grow much more quickly.

The difference it made

In 2008 TMS had sales of £224,527 and pre-tax profit of £60,770. In 2009 sales were £318,566 with a profit of £115,882.

In 2015, the combined turnover of TMS and NCASS Enterprises LLP was over £1 million and profits had grown to £213,475.

In the early days, TMS paid James, Stanley & Co. £3,775 a year for a basic service. By 2014 they were paying £11,675 for annual accounts, quarterly management accounts, Boardview (where James Stanley & Co attend their key leadership meetings as advisers), payroll, book keeping, VAT, auto enrolment set up, grant application support and tax planning.

While the numbers are impressive, the real significance is the opportunity Bob now has to work on the strategy of the company rather than having to focus on day-to-day operations. He has built up a strong management team and the company now has four directors who can manage it in his absence. In fact, he recently took a month's holiday in Spain; something he would never have been able to do previously.

Bob also now has more time to spend on the charitable causes he supports. As a committed Christian, he has adopted those principles in his business and offered job opportunities to apprentices and graduates who have previously not had employment experience.

How it made them feel

Bob is proud of the fact that he has built a successful business, both from a personal point of view and from the standpoint of his family. He is proud that his company is seen as the 'go to' organisation for mobile caterers in need of training, insurance, advice and support. Success has been hard earned; over the years Bob has put in long hours and he is relieved that finally he has achieved success.

It's a mark of the high level of support that TMS gets from James, Stanley & Co. that they actively refer them to their membership. Together, the two companies have created videos and webinars for the TMS website to help members tackle accountancy issues.

After his previous experiences, Bob was anxious about increasing his cost base and stripping away all of the company's profits when he moved from his garage into commercial offices. Andrew was able to give him peace of mind by preparing budgets that showed that the move was affordable and the company would still be in profit.

And Andrew adds, "One thing in particular makes me very proud. Bob would say that several years back he only stayed loyal to our firm because we were friends. Since we joined AVN in 2009 our service levels have gone through the roof and he now sees the firm as proactive and supportive."

Raising almost $1.5 million and creating a bright future for young with Down's syndrome

Jaques Stanmore Financial Group Pty Ltd is a 26 person practice in Brookdale, Australia that has:

- Built a hugely successful business
- Rooted itself in a 'culture of generosity'
- Generated over $1.375 million for more than 20 worthy causes
- Helped create a bright future for a young girl with Down's syndrome

"To have a purpose beyond our daily working life is both humbling and satisfying. To have that purpose together as a team is unifying and empowering," says one of the firm's founders.

Background information

This is a very different kind of case study. It is not about a single client. But is instead about how the practice has put its intent of 'Partnering 2 Prosper' at the centre of everything it does by fostering a 'culture of generosity'.

Craig Stanmore, one of the two founders, explains: "Our motivation to do this is based on two strong beliefs. Firstly, that community needs are not just the responsibility of governments, they are also the responsibility of the private sector. And secondly that accountants, by the very nature of the industry, have relationships with every business in the country and are in a position of significant influence in the private sector."

What they did

They started by making a strategic decision to concentrate their efforts on the following areas:

1. Helping the disadvantaged

2. Supporting clients who are involved in charitable activities

3. Emergency appeals – for example where assistance is needed urgently due to natural disasters

4. Business related charities – to help others through business vehicles such as micro loans

5. Patron arrangements – where members of their team had a special connection with or passion for a particular charity

The difference they made

Examples of the specific things they have done, and the difference it has made, include:

- **Giving more than $1.375 million through The Jaques Stanmore Foundation** – a charitable trust they founded in 2009 with 'deductible gift recipient' status (ie donations to it are tax deductible). This has been funded by 1-1.5% of the turnover of the practice, along with donations from clients and the team.

- **An annual Jaques Stanmore Foundation Award** – given to a team member who the partners consider would be enriched by an experience of serving others less fortunate.

- **Monthly "Mufti Days"** – where the team nominates a charity to raise funds for on the day.

- **Helping refugees and others start small businesses in Sulewesi** – two of the partners personally visited a micro loan organisation there, gave small group business training to its loan officers and loan recipients to help them provide an income and a future for their families, and the firm now also provides ongoing financial support to the organisation itself.

- **Supporting Anglicare's 'Toys'n Tucker' annual collection** – with their team bringing in gifts and food for Christmas hampers.

- **Quarterly Blood Bank donations** – arranged by the firm for a large number of team members and partners.

- **Honorary work** – Partners, in particular, do honorary work for a number of "not for profit" organisations, and are involved on charitable boards for churches, schools etc.

- **Regularly bringing in speakers from charity organisations** – to address all those gathered at the firm's weekly team meetings.

How it made them feel

Quotes from the letters of thanks and appreciation they have received include:

- "Your support …. has been greatly appreciated and has enabled Lifestart to support families who care for a child living with disability or development delay."

- "Because of your vision and generosity in supporting the work that we do, we have been able to continue to offer free world class debt counselling to the community."

- "A child is born with cerebral palsy in Australia every 15 hours… and without the generosity of people just like you we simply couldn't meet the demand."

- "Your generous gift will make us successful in the fight against all women's cancers."

According to Craig, "Our business has also benefited in many different ways. But perhaps the most significant way is the positive impact it has all had on our team culture. To have a purpose beyond our daily working life is both humbling and satisfying. To have that purpose together as a team is unifying and empowering."

And it is paying off commercially too, since the firm now has a leadership team of five partners and managers supported by 21 professionals and support team members, weathered the recession really well and continues to enjoy rapid growth. All of which is excellent for a practice that was only started in 1994.

A very personal letter of proof

What follows is all unedited text of an inspiring letter of thanks from one of the firm's clients, Andrew Wilson and his daughter Grace:

"ACCOUNTING WITH GRACE AND COMPASSION – THANK YOU

With FY2015/16 underway, I think this will be our 11th year of working together, so a quick note of appreciation – a testimonial for you to share.

As the years roll on I am giving you even more of my tax, admin, banking, planning and accounting. The more I give to you, the less of this stuff I do myself and the more time I have for things that I would prefer to be doing.

We started in 2005, with a referral from my solicitor, shortly after my first child – Grace – was born. I was living overseas, and you advised, assisted me to establish, and now help me to run and keep compliant a Family Trust. I am a professional Non Executive Director and consultant. The Family Trust structure allows me to secure assets of my family, and protect them against the unlikely event of a legal action against me personally. It is also a useful vehicle for giving, and most importantly a way of providing a place for long term financial security for my daughter Grace, who has Down's syndrome. Grace is in year 4 at our local school and has a wonderful future before her. We have a plan, and [you at] JSFG are part of the plan.

Next, I asked you to do the accounting for my consulting company. This has grown to accounting and compliance. And bookkeeping. Plus, as much of the admin as I can pass over to you as well.

Next, I sought Sook's [one of the partners] advice and we set up a giving vehicle, with an independent board, and tax deductibility – Adil Foundation.

Next, Sook is now doing my personal tax returns, plus my wife, plus Grace.

This year I aim to reduce my admin load by going "paperless" and electronic filing. You are helping, facilitating, and with my limited IT skills, your IT people may again be called upon to guide me from time to time.

As a Non Executive Director some of my directorships are well paid commercial ones and others are Not-For-Profit. The charitable ones come with a string of interesting questions, particularly as legislation changes. JSFG never seem to charge me for these "additional questions". We work as a partnership. Thank you for helping me to help my community.

One of our best examples of partnership is Kayak For Kids (K4K), a kayak paddle from the Sydney Harbour Bridge to Clontarf, and Lifestart's biggest fundraiser.

Grace received early intervention from Lifestart from age 3-6 and it has set her up to attend our local school in an integrated setting, and hopefully that will continue into High School and life.

We are so appreciative of Lifestart that most years we still help fundraise with K4K. Funds raised for my boat receive "matched giving" from Adil Foundation. JSFG are a generous firm that has always made significant gifts to Lifestart via my boat on K4K -- and isn't it great synergy when Jaques Stanmore Foundation – your Foundation to help the community gives a donation and that is doubled by Adil Foundation, *which you helped me set up. The "matched giving" is a big incentive to other givers, and you have enabled that through Adil.*

In my opinion, supporting our community through efficient and effective giving of time and money, is made possible through good structures and generous people – thank you for both!

Looking forward to the next 11 years."

A charity let down by their accountant gets a vital lifeline

A sole practitioner with a team of four based in Derry, Northern Ireland who has helped:

- To save a small charity that was months away from closure
- Retain six jobs and create a further three
- Secure guaranteed funding for the next four years
- Make the charity more attractive to other funding bodies

"This was all about the positive impact we could make on a small charity," the practitioner says. "Providing what they needed, when they needed it, was the true benefit to our firm."

Background information

Something Special is a small charity operating in the north west region of Northern Ireland. Founded in 2007, they provide educational and social opportunities to 120 young people and adults with learning difficulties, including educational programmes, social events and the encouragement of creative expression to develop confidence. The charity is an integral part of the local community.

The situation at the start

The charity is reliant on external funding to keep going and in January 2015 they needed to apply for new funding from the European Social Fund to secure their future for the next four years. Without this finance, the charity would have to close down within a matter of months.

A key part of the application was to produce an up-to-date income and expenditure report, but none of the team had the necessary accountancy skills to prepare this properly. So they naturally turned to their existing accountants as they knew and trusted them to help with this vital and urgent document.

The response was shocking – "We can't help you. We're just too busy doing tax returns."

So the charity faced closure simply because their accountants hadn't planned effectively for tax return season.

How their accountants helped

The charity administrator had previously worked with K. Phelan & Co. in his own business and he contacted Kieran to see if he could help.

At this point, it's best to explain how Kieran handles tax returns.

"Our firm has a simple policy. We insist on all books and records being submitted to our office by 30th September each year for the previous tax year, so that all tax returns are completed and submitted by 30th November.

"I personally spent 12 years in other practices repeating the same cycle over and over again. We would complete approximately 75% of our annual workload in one month – January. Coming back to the office after the Christmas holidays was not a nice experience. We would be knuckling down to working 12 hours a day, 7 days a week, all to compensate either our own poor practices throughout the rest of the year, or to deal with clients who always left things to the last minute.

"When I started my own firm in 2010, I made a decision to break the mould in a number of ways, one being that we would not be working overtime in January. It's now our policy and part of our terms and conditions that the deadline for tax returns is 30th November. All our clients know this and they are fully on board. So we don't need to dread January anymore!"

This approach means that the team are free to deal with their own business development during December and January, bringing in new systems or improving processes and procedures. And they also have the time to look at adding value to clients and to actively seek new clients, at a time when the majority of other firms simply don't have the time to do it.

"So we had no problem helping the charity in January 2015," Kieran explains. "Over the course of three days, we worked with the administrator to help utilise the charity's spreadsheet based payments/ receipts records and construct a bank reconciliation statement for all bank accounts covering from the last year end date up to the end of December 2014."

They also obtained the previous accounts from the administrator and reviewed and accounted for debtors and creditors and computed the depreciation charge.

The difference it made

The charity was able to submit their funding application within the deadline and a few weeks later they contacted Kieran again.

"We were delighted to hear that the application for funding was successful! The charity was granted £280,000 which secured their existence for another four years."

The impact was profound:

- Six full-time jobs were retained in the charity and a further three posts were also created.

- A total of 120 students (i.e. adults with learning difficulties) will take part in the charity's projects over the next three years. This means that each year an average of 30 adults with learning difficulties will be able to achieve qualifications that will enable them to benefit from social inclusion and achieve recognition of their educational and creative achievements in a truly meaningful way.

- The charity can now bring in volunteers from secondary schools to help young people learn the skills needed to work with adults with learning difficulties.

- A local school has given use of its premises free of charge for the next year, so the charity has better facilities for its students.

"I went to meet the founder of the charity and the administrator soon after the news broke that the funding application was successful," Kieran says. "We discussed how we could now implement a cloud accounting system which would dramatically improve their financial reporting procedures for the future.

"The founder of the charity couldn't thank us enough for what we had done for them and how quickly and efficiently we had helped them in their hour of need."

How it made them feel

After being let down so badly by their existing accountants, the charity was extremely grateful for Kieran's help.

In fact, they appointed K. Phelan as their new accountants with a fee for cloud accounting training as well as annual compliance.

The charity believes that they are not only much better placed to obtain new funding from the European Social Fund in the future, but that they will also be able to attract new funding from other providers.

Kieran is equally delighted. "The closure of Something Special would have meant the loss of highly valuable and needed services for those adults challenged by learning difficulties, something which would have affected one of the most vulnerable sections of our society locally and have a devastating impact on their day-to-day lives and their prospects for the future.

"In particular, the volunteering from secondary schools that's now possible will help increase and improve awareness in our society of the challenges faced by adults with learning difficulties. Despite their challenges, these adults are no different to you and I and they deserve the same opportunities and life-chances as everyone else."

"My accountant helped me build not just a business, but a family too"

A four director firm with a team of 16 based in Cardiff, Wales, which has helped a client:

- Avoid bankruptcy
- Develop a hugely successful business that is also compatible with family life
- Turned losses into a profit of £447,280
- Realise their dream of creating a cutting edge health and wellness centre for Wales

The client describes their impact as "totally above and beyond what an accountant is expected to give."

Background information

Ben Mathew is a chiropractor working in Cardiff. Originally introduced to chiropractic after a back injury, his ambitious goal is to enable the health of tens of thousands of people and inspire others with his passion for chiropractic care. He is married to Izzy, who also works for the business.

The situation at the start

Initially Ben was in partnership with another chiropractor, but the situation was far from ideal:

- He had signed a personal guarantee for a three year lease on a building that wasn't really suitable for their purpose

- They had no established patient list

- They had no financial systems

- There were no marketing strategies in place

- And no bank borrowing facility either

As a result, the partnership could not continue, and Ben faced personal bankruptcy.

The first thing Neil Ballard of Lewis Ballard did was to stabilise things by extracting Ben from the partnership and forming a new limited company so the lease could be renegotiated without the personal guarantee. He also secured an overdraft facility for the business.

The emotional impact of the predicament on Ben was significant. He was deeply hurt by the partnership problems and his confidence was seriously diminished. But his passion for chiropractic remained and his determination to succeed prevailed. So, with a loan from his parents, he decided to continue in business alone.

Initially he needed lots of support and guidance, with regular meetings and calls as Neil advised how to build up the business and recommended treatment plans and referral schemes to ensure repeat business and further growth.

By October 2009 the business had expanded to the extent that new premises with additional treatment rooms and an x-ray room were needed and also potentially another chiropractor to assist Ben. On Neil's advice, Izzy, Ben's wife, left her secure teaching job to work full time in the business.

How their accountants helped - Part 1

Although business was booming there were underlying issues that meant Ben and Izzy were paying a high personal cost for their success. They were each working over 60 hours a week and the strain was affecting their physical and mental wellbeing.

So in October 2010 Neil invited them to a Lewis Ballard Focus day to try to move forwards. The Focus Day identified their key issues as:

- The business was not fully systemised so it was very dependent on Ben and Izzy being there
- They lacked management systems so it was difficult to measure and manage the business
- Izzy lacked confidence and experience in managing team issues
- Quarterly financial reporting was no longer adequate as the business grew

- There was no clear vision or purpose for the business that the team and patients could believe in

- Internal communication was poor and the business goals hadn't been shared with the team

- They lacked knowledge of the market and their competitors

- Ben found it uncomfortable to collect money from patients and gave too much away for free to avoid embarrassment. Debtors were also becoming a problem.

Neil and the team from Lewis Ballard:

- Recommended that they reviewed the current team requirements, recruitment processes, job roles and training systems to develop a highly skilled and motivated team who were clear on what was expected and were confident to work without supervision. They also discussed how personal profiling could help find the right candidate for each job and showed them sample job roles.

- Encouraged Izzy to prioritise time to immediately implement systems. As a result she quickly set up some of the key processes and straightaway the clinic began to run more efficiently.

- Discussed at length the business manager role, helping Izzy to understand that she was entitled to want the best out of their business and should not be afraid to hold people accountable. As it was a new role she was going to experience some resistance, but in time she would gain trust and respect. They gave her advice on how to deal with issues constructively and very quickly Izzy grew into her new role and was accepted by their team.

- Trained Izzy on cloud accounting software to produce monthly management figures so they could be reviewed to monitor progress and maintain control.

- Helped to develop a draft mission statement. Once finalised this formed the basis of the clinic's message, ethos and core values.

- Recommended regular team meetings to improve communication. Team members were encouraged to suggest improvements to systems or services, as they are best placed to assess where improvements can be made. They also supplied template feedback forms and suggested how to hold open meetings to encourage team spirit, participation and ideas. This resulted in a much greater team buy in.

- Benchmarked the business to gain insights into the market and competition. They also supplied a template patient survey to help measure satisfaction and indicate areas for improvement or new services that could be provided.

- De-personalised the payment of fees by suggesting that a price list was drawn up and adhered to. They also proposed creating a job sheet for any extra services, so they could be priced at the time of consultation but with the receptionist collecting the fees. This would help to avoid any costly gestures of kindness from Ben (something which had been a frequent and expensive issue in the past!). This immediately improved cash flow and almost simultaneously eliminated bad debt. The use of treatment plans and bundles also helped to ensure regular cash flow.

How their accountants helped - Part 2

Ben and Izzy had great plans for the business and wanted to develop additional services such as x-rays, orthotics, yoga and exercise classes. However, the business was still very reliant on them personally, and until the new systems and team were fully in place, they simply didn't have the capacity to cope with extra business.

The Focus Day also highlighted the fact that they both wanted to start a family, but were anxious about how that would combine with the business. Neil reassured them that it was possible to have both, if they implemented the recommended changes.

Ben explained: "I didn't know what to expect but this was the most valuable day of my life – both for my business and personally."

As a result of the Focus Day, Ben and Izzy started to build a business that wasn't so reliant on them being there. But there were still some rocky times ahead...

Ben had taken on another chiropractor to free up his time for studying, developing cutting edge treatments and raising the profile of the business. However, eventually he had to be let go. This led to an unsuccessful but traumatic tribunal claim. Neil put them in touch with their own advisers who supported them through the tribunal and gave ongoing support with health and safety and employment law.

Recruitment of another associate was under way when Ben and Izzy announced that they were expecting their first child in July 2011. Although this made recruitment even more imperative, progress was slow. Ben decided that he would prefer to increase efficiencies and see more patients himself and then bring in an associate later in the year. So once again, the business became dependent on Ben.

The situation was brought sharply into focus when the baby was born in May, three months prematurely. With a child in the neo-natal unit, Izzy was suddenly unable to manage the business and Ben's time was divided between the clinic and hospital.

For many months the family focus was on their child's health and time was consumed with a string of hospital appointments. However, due to the systems in place, the team pulling together and the strong loyalty of patients, the business survived this very difficult period. The treatment plans that had been implemented meant that patients remained loyal and payment methods ensured cash-flow maintained a healthy level.

Throughout this time, Lewis Ballard provided support to keep the business on track and gave guidance and friendship to help Ben and Izzy cope.

It took until June 2012 to find a suitable associate to join the business. Once he was in position and able to take on new referrals, Ben and Izzy's dream of a one-stop health and wellness centre became a real possibility.

And when they found a listed period building that was ideal for conversion, Neil helped them to acquire funding, recommended solicitors and specialist surveyors, and also saved them £60,000 on their tax bill so they could purchase the property.

As is the way with most building projects, the costs of the repairs escalated and Neil provided guidance, as well as helping them to raise further funding to complete the project and maximising further tax savings of £128,000 (through a Business Premises Renovation Allowance claim).

As a result, they proudly opened the doors of their state of the art new centre in January 2015.

The difference it made

In financial terms the impact on the business was huge:

- Accounts for September 2007 showed a loss of £25,000
- September 2008 - £27,000 net profit
- September 2009 - £132,618 net profit
- September 2010 - £191,264 net profit

- September 2012 - £229,922 net profit
- By 2014 net profit had reached £447,280

Turnover is currently more each month than for the whole of the first year, with monthly average takings for the first six months in their new clinic reaching £76,501. Their cash-flow is excellent.

Professionally they are now the leading clinic in Wales, employing eight people, and are developing a training programme to help graduates build their dream practices, so they too can inspire and change the health system in Wales.

Personally, Ben and Izzy have recently purchased their dream home and are now the proud parents of two beautiful children. They are both millionaires in their own right and have a financially secure future.

Lewis Ballard earn regular annual fees of £5,500 from the relationship, with additional projects averaging approximately £2000 in most years. The firm's family and friends are regularly treated by Ben and Neil says, "The difference to our health has been amazing. They have become friends and we have become their most trusted advisors. They always refer to us and always give us credit whenever possible."

Perhaps even more significantly, when this story was told by Neil and Ben live on stage in September 2015 the delegates at the AVN National Accountants Conference voted Lewis Ballard as "The UK's Most Inspiring Accountants". And along with the title, they also received a £10,000 cash prize sponsored by Xero.

As for Ben, over the years his standing and reputation as a chiropractor has grown dramatically and he is seen as a bright star of the profession, who passionately champions the benefits of chiropractic care. In 2014 he attended an international chiropractic conference in Toronto and was awarded the international Chiropractic Community Rising Star award. In October 2015 he received the international UCA Chiropractor of the year award and has been invited to be the opening speaker at the next conference in 2016.

How it made them feel

The emotional impact has been even greater than the financial impact.

As Ben and Izzy wrote to Neil, "What you do goes from basic accounting to life coaching – totally above and beyond what an accountant is expected to give. I don't have small aspirations and my wife and I are so glad that we have you in our lives as we have never taken a backward step in our business or private life in the time that we have known you. All that we have is because of you. You are really very special."

Taking an online start-up accountancy practice to $1m in a year and a half

LiveCA LLP is a two owner, 13 person firm based in Canada that has harnessed technology to:

- Build a $1m business within 18 months of starting up
- Eliminate the need for an office
- Recruit "top of the class" talent
- Pay above average salaries
- Earn above average profits
- Provide flexible lifestyle choices for the entire team

"It's been an extremely rewarding and exciting journey," says partner Chad Davis.

Background information

LiveCA was founded three years ago, and is owned by Chad Davis CPA, CMA, MBA and Josh Zweig, CPA, CA, LPA. Although they have a postal address in Toronto, in reality none of the team works at that address because the business is 100% online.

When we interviewed them they had a long list of stories of how they had impacted the lives of their customers. But we have chosen to focus instead on the story of the firm itself, since we believe it will inspire many other accountants to see what is possible when you run a truly 21st century practice.

In many senses it provides a blueprint for how to rise to all of the main challenges facing the profession, including:

- Harnessing technology – rather than being destroyed by it
- Providing world class service
- Recruiting talented people

- Winning high quality clients

- Being rewarded financially and emotionally

- Achieving an optimal work-life integration

The situation at the start

Four years ago Chad was working in the Cayman Islands for an international group of companies and Josh was working for a traditional accounting firm. Chad was extremely frustrated by the practical difficulties of extracting the information central management needed from the group's many different desktop accounting systems around the world, and Josh knew there had to be a better way to serve clients.

Then in 2010, Chad came across cloud accounting. "It changed everything," he says. "And because no one was really doing much with Xero in Canada, I spent a year researching and building up the courage until I was ready to leave my job, move my family away from the beach and back to snowy Canada, and start an exclusively online practice." The situation was similar for Josh. He started offering services over Skype and grew his customer base over the coming months.

Within a few months Chad's firm was at the top of the Xero partner listing in Canada. "At that point Josh contacted me online, and we started passing work to each other because he specialised in tax and I didn't. It was incredibly hard to find a CPA that was willing to learn a new system," explained Chad. "We soon realized that with complementary, but completely different skill sets, we had a chance to build a firm that had a shot at building something truly great. But because we work exclusively online, the first time we actually met was when Josh flew to Halifax, Nova Scotia to meet me to work on developing our partnership agreement!"

What they did

"Being a virtual practice in itself is not anything special," says Chad. "But what makes it game-changing is how we have also focussed on building a practice driven by customer needs, not pricing based on a menu and not being closed minded on the services we'll offer. Through this we spent a lot of time on processes, documenting as much as we can, systematically learning from every failure, and involving everybody in the firm in constantly improving every single aspect of what we do. Because of that we are able to attract the very best people, wherever they are located in the country. It's really rewarding working next to people who believe the same things you believe and work tirelessly every day to make the lives of our customers better."

This approach can be seen in many of the specific keys to their success, including:

- **Semi-annual firm retreats** – At the first of these events they focused on Simon Sinek's seminal book, "Start with why", and used it to identify and articulate their core purpose. And at the second they focused for four days on how best to apply the systemisation principles of Michael Gerber's "E-Myth Revisited". Interestingly, these retreats are the only times most of their team members have actually physically met.

- **Learning from the gurus** – "Simon's 'Start with why' and Michael's 'E-myth revisited', along with Ron Baker's "Implementing value pricing", are the pillars at the foundation of the firm. And a new favourite of ours is Warren Berger's "A More Beautiful Question". We don't agree with absolutely every detail on every page, but they contain so much we do agree with, and they are fundamental to our success," says Chad.

- **Everybody has a say** – "The entire team is literally EXPECTED, and not merely allowed, to be involved in making the business the best it can be. Everybody has a voice, everybody is listened to, and every contribution is valued."

- **After Action Reviews** – As part of their "sometimes you win and sometimes you learn" philosophy, they carry out 'After Action Reviews' every time something goes well or badly. And those reviews are shared in real time with the entire team via the app Slack, so that they learn every lesson and build every nuance of best practice into their systems. "They are also incredibly valuable for new team members to review to see why we do certain things the way we do."

- **Access to the entire client relationship** – "Even our most junior team members are fully engaged because they know they can make an impact on the entire client relationship. All they have to do is show initiative. Nothing is off limits to them and in return, they know they will be rewarded with appreciation, feedback, experience and career growth."

- **Quarterly client meetings** – "Although most customers come to LiveCA because the technology and processes we introduce solve some of their immediate pain points, the real value comes in the form of quarterly management meetings where we get to learn about the owner's plan for the business. We support that call with financial information and the result is usually a great relationship that grows the more we learn from each other."

- **Emotionally connected team** – "Everybody in the team has an emotional connection with the business because they really believe in what we're doing. They are here for the profession: to push forward what customers think of accountants as a whole and they know they are changing those perceptions every single day."

- **Giving back to the profession** – Because of their deep rooted belief that they are there for the profession, they are always willing to explain what they have learned with other accountants. As a result they are frequently invited to share their experiences at major accountancy conferences, and often share their systems, documents and procedures on a one-to-one basis with other practitioners.

The step by step process at the heart of their success

"Companies usually come to us because they think they need help with tax or their accounts. But we flip the conversation around from the very beginning, because we know that an even more important (but unrecognised) issue is that they don't know what they want to get out of a good system and rarely consider the entire lifecycle of data in the context of decision making. Our intention is to find out exactly what information is required to support the things that are important to them, and without a good system for that it'd be pretty tough."

This approach is formalised in the five step process they use with all new clients.

Step 1: Discovery – This is done via a structured and comprehensive online meeting with one of the CPAs. The aim is to identify their goals and aspirations, and then drill down into an analysis of what they really need. As part of this they also explain their approach to customer service to see if it's a good fit for the potential customer.

Step 2: There's an app for that – This technical demonstration step is usually carried out by a member of the technical team, who are all accountants with deep technical accounting backgrounds. "Every single potential customer has a unique story and it's in this phase of the discovery process that we fine tune what they find valuable, how we can structure the accounting processes appropriately to aid in delivering that value and show them exactly how we're going to do it. It's easy for most people to find an app online, receive technical support for free and try on their own so it's important that people see value in us more than just the apps we use, but the methodology behind our technical approach to solving problems. Apps come and apps go, but as long as they know their interests are at the heart of each recommendation we'll be on the right path."

Step 3: Value pricing – LiveCA then offers clients a choice of three customised options, each of which includes all the necessary year-end accounts and tax compliance work. "We price every customer individually, so the services delivered can differ greatly from customer to customer. Value pricing is hard work and you don't always get it right; but the more you practice the better you get. Prices are always presented during a video chat and we walk them through each of the packages to make sure they're aware of all the important elements of each option so they're fully prepared to decide which one is the best fit."

Step 4: Kick-off – "This is an online call where we'll set up all of the systems, wrap up the admin, and introduce them to the LiveCA team they will work with. That three person team always consists of a Chartered Professional Accountant (not a partner) for high level tax and accounting support, a technical adviser to sort out the technology, and an associate for the day to day details. They work alongside the client throughout the relationship, and get to know them intimately."

Step 5: The Work Begins – "In this step we teach them how to use all their new apps, and help them to develop a workflow that makes sense. As part of this we create step by step checklists and procedure documents for them, and have them follow a homework schedule. And, on an ongoing basis, they have unlimited access to their accounting team using their preferred contact methods (Skype, Google Hangouts, email, etc)."

It's a process that the team really believe in, because as senior manager Greg Toner explains, "There are countless opportunities to create value for clients through the proper use of technology combined with a strong tax and accounting knowledge base."

Key technology

Some of the technology LiveCA finds most useful in helping them to run an online practice includes:

- Slack – for helping team members communicate and cut down on the volume of email
- WorkflowMax – for managing firm recurring jobs, leads and customer information

- ScheduleOnce – for booking in meetings that require pooled availability

- RightSignature – for signing electronic documents

- Google Apps – for email, calendar and collaborative documents

- RecruiterBox – to manage incoming resumes and job postings

- Teamwork Desk – for technical helpdesk support (internally and externally)

In addition, some of the apps that their clients find most useful include:

- Xero and QuickBooks Online – for the core accounting tasks

- Receipt Bank & HubDoc – for processing purchases and automatically retrieving bank statements

- Crunchboards – for providing flexible management dashboards

- Payline by ICE, Rotessa, TransferMate and Plooto – for online payment management

- Dear Inventory – for inventory tracking and sales

- Shopify – for ecommerce and point of sale systems

The difference it made

This approach has allowed LiveCA to:

- Grow into a $1million practice within 18 months of starting up

- Earn well above average profits

- Turn 85% of the prospects who they price into customers

- Work with customers from anywhere in Canada

- Create 11 new jobs

- Recruit top in class talent, regardless of where they happen to live

- Pay above average salaries

- Avoid the need for an expensive office, and instead only pay $100 a month for an accommodation address service

- Hold all their meetings with clients online. "And those meetings tend to be shorter and much more focused. So they greatly improve our productivity too. In fact, the only time we ever meet clients in person is if we accidentally bump into them at a social event!"

- Have team members working from home in five different Canadian provinces, and
- Allow the two partners to live wherever they want (at the time of writing they live over 4500km apart).

How it made them feel

"It was tough at first and we were working long hours. But we didn't mind because we have always believed we're helping build something truly great. We realise that we are enabling a new type of firm to exist, and the freedom that allows in our personal lives is well worth the extra hours," explains Chad.

Little by little, of course, things got better and he is now able to take his daughter to school in the morning, put both of his children to bed in the evening, and keep weekends completely free for family time. Josh also enjoys travelling and working from locations all around the world. "Life is good," says Josh.

According to Chad, "It's been an extremely rewarding and exciting journey from initial chaos to eventual order because we now have the right people performing the right roles. Our goal is now to become a profitable firm that provides a challenging and rewarding work environment for everyone that wants to come along for the ride. Although we have high hopes and goals for the firm, we'd like to get there the right way, not straying from our core values of enriching the lives of our employees and customers in everything we do. To do this, we are reinvesting most of our profits in people, technology and systems to get there even faster."

Josh explains, "When I originally set out to pursue my CPA designation, it was so that I could gain a skill to make an impact on the businesses where I'd work and launch an exciting career. LiveCA is an extension of that passion to make an impact in the lives of others, but also in a way that challenges the general accountant stigma and makes us proud to be CPAs." Josh leads the tax and compliance side of the firm and originally came up with the name LiveCA.

Other members of the LiveCA team put it like this:

- "I wanted to help revitalise an industry that really, really needed a reboot. I love helping people out and teaching them new things or new ways to do old things." Dave MacPherson, Technical Director

- "LiveCA is a trailblazing company that welcomes innovation with open arms. It allows me to draw from all the hats I've worn in my career in order to serve clients, and contribute ideas. Also, after breaking two snow-shovels digging my car out from under 13 feet of snow last winter, working from home is a massive bonus." Leigh Sheppard, Onboarding Associate

- "Every day I look forward to working with our amazing team, always searching for new ways to improve the lives of our clients and ourselves." Jeff Kelly, Associate

- "After several years with a national firm, the search for a home that put me in a position to add value for clients day-in, day-out led me to LiveCA's doorstep. Being part of a group that understands technology and leverages it in almost everything we do, all with the goal of improving both our clients' lives and our own, is what continues to draw me in. After that, having the flexibility to work from anywhere is just a bonus!" Tyler Bradley, CPA CA Senior Manager

Saving a business owner and his family from embarrassment

Michelle Long is a sole practitioner based in Missouri, USA, who helped a client:

- Identify why gross margins kept falling
- Stop a cash flow crisis destroying the business
- Prevent his brother losing the substantial investment he had made in the business
- Save him and his family from embarrassment

"Not only does that make me feel wonderful, but it is also really helping my business to grow," says Michelle.

Background information

Sam's Sandwich Shops (name changed to preserve confidentiality) was opened in two locations under a franchise agreement by two brothers (we will call them Andy and Steve).

Neither of them had any experience operating a franchise or a restaurant. Steve was a former NFL (National Football League) football player, and so provided most of the funding. But he lived out of state and was not involved in the daily operations. So Andy managed both locations.

The situation at the start

Michelle explained, "Every month I would call Andy to schedule a time to discuss the financial statements with him. Initially he looked forward to our meetings to see how the locations were performing. But soon he became so busy that when it was time for our monthly meeting he would keep cancelling. And instead he assured me he would look at the financials later."

Rather than let it slip, Michelle started using QuickBooks to monitor the numbers on her own until suddenly she noticed the gross profit margin had declined at one of the locations. There was no obvious reason for the decline – sales appeared steady, supplier prices hadn't increased and there were no apparent changes in operations or other obvious causes. "The following month gross margins fell again. I was concerned and tried to discuss it with Andy to no avail. He was still too busy to listen."

This went on for several months. Gross margins kept falling, and Andy kept being too busy to even talk about it.

How their accountants helped

"I didn't give up", explains Michelle, "and eventually the declining gross margins started affecting profits and cash flow so much that it became difficult to pay all the bills. So I was finally able to get Andy's attention."

They met and Michelle explained the various factors that could result in a decline in gross profit margin, including:

- Sales not being captured – employees not ringing up sales etc.

- Sales being under-reported – ringing up a 'small' and serving a 'large' etc.

- Higher costs from waste – not storing food properly, not making meals properly etc.

- Suppliers increasing their prices

- Stock being stolen

"Before that conversation Andy had no idea what was happening or what could be causing it. But now he knew exactly what to look for, and he very quickly discovered two employees stealing cases of meat and lots of other expensive food, by simply taking it out the back door."

The difference it made

Michelle's perseverance and input resulted in:

- The thieves being fired

- Profitability returning to normal, and

- The jobs of everyone being saved, since if the theft had continued and cash flow had got worse, the business wouldn't have survived much longer

How it made them feel

"Initially Andy was very stressed and busy, so he didn't make time to listen to me properly. It's almost as if he thought any problems would magically solve themselves without any effort on his part."

"But because I persevered, he realised (just in time) the vital importance of working in tandem with his accountant as a trusted advisor to monitor the key numbers, and acting upon the issues they raise."

"To us, as accountants, spotting falling margins, and the advice I gave about potential causes are probably glaringly obvious. But most clients don't have that kind of knowledge. So even though we often think that what we have to say is common sense, they usually find it massively valuable."

"And for Andy it really was massively valuable, because it prevented him losing his business and avoiding the embarrassment of losing the money that his brother had invested in it. So he has become one of our best sources of referrals, and is always quick to tell everyone what a great 'adviser and partner' I am."

"Not only does that make me feel wonderful, but it is also really helping my business to grow."

Growing into a 120 person firm because they really care for each other

LUMENROCK is a seven director South African firm with 12 offices that has:

- Helped young people who couldn't afford a professional education become business leaders
- Created a genuinely caring culture
- Grown into a 120 person firm in less than 15 years

Background information

Pieter Esterhuizen started his practice in 2003 on a farm in a remote part of South Africa near Vrede. Today he is the managing director of a firm with 12 offices, two of which are overseas, and a team of 120 people. This is the story of how he has changed the lives of the young people who have been on the journey with him.

How they helped

After being introduced to Simon Sinek's seminal book "Start with why", the firm recently did some very deep and honest thinking to identify their "why" which they then articulated as "Because we care, we make a difference". And that focus on caring is not just a new slogan. It has always been fundamental to the success and growth of the firm and is self-evident in how they treat their people.

Six of Pieter's first seven employees are still with the firm. None of them came from a privileged background. None of them had more than a general school education. And none of them could really afford relevant professional education or training.

Nevertheless, Pieter decided to give them a chance. So as well as offering them jobs, in-house training and support, he also offered them bursaries to fund their professional education.

The difference it has made

When the firm opened a major new office 1200 km away in George in Western Cape, all six of them relocated there with Pieter. And as the business has flourished, so have their careers:

- Brenda, who had no background in accountancy and started as a receptionist, is now the Office Manager in George, the largest office in the group

- Wilma, who also started as a receptionist, is now senior bookkeeper

- Wynand, Wilma's son, who started as a part-time messenger, is now the Financial Manager for the entire group

- Armand, Wilma's second son, who joined straight from school, is now a "roving manager" training new offices and troubleshooting in whichever office needs him most

- Ronel, who later married Wynand, is now the manager of the division that manages all the core monthly accounting services

- Peter, who is still only in his mid-20s, is now the Production Manager for the group, and is also their most senior technical accountant, apart from the partners

The firm also has an annual "Employee Of The Year" prize, which is awarded using an objective scoring scheme based on the firm's "Five star performance standards". The prize is open to all 120 employees, but for the last four years it has been won by Armand, Peter, Wynand and Ronel. "For the last two years," Pieter explained, "I withdrew from the final decision making in the prize giving process so that no one could think I was favouring my original six employees. The truth is they have all been worthy winners, and have won their prizes and their promotions entirely on merit."

In the same way that the original six employees have grown as professionals, the practice has enjoyed equally impressive growth. From Pieter's humble beginnings as a start-up working out of his farm, he now leads a business with 12 offices and seven directors.

How it made them feel

"I am incredibly proud that we have created a genuine team culture of caring for, supporting and valuing each other. And I'm sure they share my pride," says Pieter. "I'm also incredibly proud that I've now been asked to explain our culture at several high-profile conferences. And I'm proud that my wife Claudine, who has known my six original employees since our days back on the farm, is a kind of surrogate mother to the whole happy family.

"The dramatic increase in our size has been due to both organic growth and mergers. But our caring culture has undoubtedly been a key ingredient in our success. Because of it we have an incredibly loyal team, who really care about delivering the five-star service that gives us a great reputation and attracts a lot of new clients. In addition, their willingness to always go the extra mile for us and our clients has also allowed us to deal with the inevitable stresses and strains on our resources, systems and structure that have been caused by our rapid growth." Pieter also stressed that, "it is important to note that our other employees have also embraced this culture of loyalty, five-star service and caring, and that my co-directors also play a very large part in this success story."

Pieter also wanted to share another aspect of their team culture that makes him very proud. "A couple of years ago I heard about a 27 year old lady who had been profoundly deaf since birth, and consequently had never had a job. So we approached her parents, and offered to take her on to see if we could train her. I am proud to say that she is now a really valuable member of our support team, and that a couple of months ago we were also able to help fund a cochlear implant to help her get some a sense of sound."

"She has been such an inspiration to everyone in the firm. We have all learned so much from her about having the right attitude, determination and commitment. We have learned to appreciate all the talents and circumstances we have been dealt in life. And we have all become happier and even more caring as a result."

A journey from the brink of insolvency to profits of more than £100,000

McKellens, a two-director firm with a team of twelve, based in Stockport, England, which has helped a client:

- Avoid insolvency and save 16 jobs
- Turn losses of £200,000 into profits of £100,000
- Bring the company out of the bank's 'special measures' and back into mainstream banking
- Finance the purchase of a £200,000 machine and expand their customer base

"I honestly don't know what we would have done without the support and guidance of our accountant," says the client. "We would have struggled to keep going."

Background information

Print Search Chester Ltd. (trading as PSC Systems) provides print management, direct mail and fulfilment and is a leading provider of personalised plastic cards. PSC currently employs 16 people and has a turnover of around £2million.

The situation at the start

When PSC first met McKellens they had recently lost a major customer and as result their turnover had decreased by a third. The directors had no regular management information and didn't react quickly enough to the change in their income levels. Consequently they were making losses of £200,000 on turnover of £2 million.

They were struggling with a £400,000 overdraft facility and juggling payments to the taxman, suppliers and their employees in order to keep the company going. They were only able to manage the business by way

116

of seeing what was in the bank account (or not) and how close they were to their overdraft limit.

The directors were fearful that the business would be forced into insolvency and their personal guarantees called in.

How their accountants helped

McKellens took a three step approach:

- The first step was to establish credibility in the numbers coming out of the accounting system. This proved to be a challenge as the accounting system was difficult to use and did not provide any meaningful management reports. The challenge was made more difficult by the fact that year-end adjustments had not been processed properly and that no one had actually questioned whether the balances being reported were real and supported by underlying assets and liabilities.

- Once a 'clean' opening position had been ascertained the next step was to produce accurate and meaningful monthly management accounts, which the company had never had. McKellens also explained to the directors what the numbers really meant, and what impact they would have on cashflow and managing the business going forward. In effect, the firm became the virtual finance director as the directors of the company did not have a trained financial background.

- The third stage was to help to instigate a budgeting / forecasting model to give the directors a 12 month view of what was going to happen to the business from a profit, cashflow and balance sheet perspective. This model has been continuously revised to reflect the changing nature of the business and is still in use today.

In addition, McKellens also:

- Attended monthly board meetings and meetings with the company's bankers to explain what progress was being made and what the prognosis for the business was.

- Changed the basis of the directors' (who were the shareholders) remuneration. Directors' salaries were high and a lot of tax and National Insurance was being paid by the company. McKellens reviewed the remuneration strategy and changed it to be more tax efficient.

- Helped to move the accounting records to up to date software with better reporting options. Budgets and forecasts are now embedded in the accounting software so that 'actual against forecast' and 'actual against last year' reports can be produced at the touch of a button.

- Continue to train the accounts team so they can do more of the day to day processing.

- Finally the directors were invited to join the McKellens Business Accelerator sessions (regular business growth seminars). The (now) Managing Director is benefitting from the input which the group gives together with the interactions from the other group members.

The difference it made

Not long after McKellens started working with PSC, another crisis developed when the bank placed PSC in 'special measures'. The bank wanted full management information on a monthly basis and the overdraft was even more closely monitored to check it did not exceed the bank's guidelines even if it was within the total agreed facilities. Regular monitoring visits and meetings took place at least quarterly and McKellens attended and ran these meetings with the (now) Managing Director.

At one point the bank wanted the company to take an invoice discounting facility and remove the overdraft. Due to the quality of the management information and forecasts that McKellens was now providing the bank decided not to send in reporting accountants.

The company has now been returned to mainstream banking and bank monitoring is now quarterly. It operates well within its overdraft facility and is making £100,000 profits on turnover of around £2million.

In 2014 the company was able to obtain asset finance for a new machine costing £213,000 which has enabled them to get more plastic card work from a range of different customers.

The accounts function now operates on a slimmed down basis with fewer team members and is much more efficient than previously.

The overall 'tax take' from directors' remuneration has been reduced as has the cashflow burden it was creating.

Chris Booth of McKellens explains how his firm has benefited. "During the last year we billed £15,000 covering management accounts, annual accounts, budgets and forecasts and additional work arising out of the monthly directors meeting.

"In 2015 we hosted a strategic 'day away' for the directors where we used the MindMapping technique to look at the issues and challenges facing the company over the next year or two.

"We have just taken over the payroll processing for the company and we will be doing the auto enrolment compliance, which goes alongside the payroll function when the company reaches their staging date."

How it made them feel

The company would, in all likelihood, have become insolvent with the loss of all jobs. Now, the directors are full of confidence, knowing that their accounts are in good order and that they have all the financial information they need to make good decisions. They are back in mainstream banking with the ability to borrow money for new projects, which is a great relief to them.

"There are exciting times ahead for us," says the managing director, "and I absolutely believe McKellens is responsible for that."

This accountant travelled 1600km to save a failing family business

Middel & Partners is a 10 partner practice with a team of 150 and eight offices in South Africa that has helped a client:

- Recoup losses of £500,000 per year
- Eliminate bank loans of more than £3.5 million
- Restore a sense of pride and closeness to the family
- Keep alive a business that has been in the family for 70 years
- Save 145 jobs (85 permanent and 60 seasonal)

"There's a renewed sense of energy and passion now," says the client, "and that's all down to the commitment and support of our accountant."

Background information

Rustenberg Wines is a family-run wine estate located in the South African wine region of Stellenbosch. Dating back to 1682, the estate has been in the Barlow family since 1941 and has been run by Simon Barlow since 1987, with his son, Murray, joining the business in 2012.

The situation at the start

After Simon took over the farm in 1987, he spent the next 20 years bringing the business up to date, building a new winery and importing modern, virus-free grape varieties. More than £10 million was invested, with the expectation that sales would increase as a result. Sales did rise, but costs also grew and more competition meant that they had to lower their prices.

Simon met Coenie Middel in 2010 on a trip through the Namib Desert and the pair bonded immediately. At the end of the trip Simon asked Coenie to visit the farm – even though Coenie lived 1600 km away. He mentioned that there were some issues, but Coenie had no idea of the scale of the problem until he arrived a couple of months later.

Coenie remembers, "Simon introduced me to his management team and I quickly realised that things were not what they seemed to be. After asking some pertinent questions, I realised that the family weren't getting the full story about what was actually going on in the business. Simon instructed his team to provide me with financial reports including management accounts, budgets and forecasts."

It didn't take Coenie long to uncover the seriousness of the problem.

- The business was making losses of £500,000 per year and rising

- It had depleted the family fortunes by more than £20.5 million

- Bank loans were in excess of £3.5 million

- There was a slow moving wine inventory of £2 million

- The bank was refusing to extend the facilities

"The management team was still presenting Simon with unrealistic budgets, although none of the previous 10 years' budgets had been met. I was very concerned because, putting it bluntly, Rustenberg was on the brink of collapsing."

How their accountants helped

Coenie had to break the news to Simon and his wife Rozanne. "It was devastating for them to find out the true state of the business. They were angry with themselves for not identifying the problem sooner and angry with the management team. And they were also very afraid; the family fortunes were lost, the bank was threatening foreclosure and they were on the verge of bankruptcy. They were ready to give up everything."

Simon found it hard to come to terms with the state of the business, but Coenie managed to convince him that if they worked together there was still an opportunity to save it.

"It was obvious to me from the outset that the problem at Rustenberg was that Simon was not in charge of his own business and was leaving too much in the hands of his management team. It was clearly time for Simon to get back in the driving seat."

Coenie looked at all the elements that influenced cashflow to determine which needed the most focus and initially targeted three main areas:

- Cost cutting – "I met with every team member to assess his or her roles and responsibilities, so we could see who was vital to the business and who was a drain on resources. This is never a pleasant process, but it's fundamental in rescuing a failing business. In order to be fair and thorough I brought in an HR specialist to deal with the restructuring of salaries, working closely with her during this process. The farm manager and finance manager were asked to leave immediately and Simon took charge of the farming operations and day-to-day finances with my team assisting."

- Reducing the inventory holdings – "We reduced production, cut costs and stopped the unnecessary capital expenditure. To move some of the excess inventory we discounted the slow moving stock and were able to sell it in a very short space of time."

- Regaining the confidence of the bank – "Communication with financial bodies is often all it takes to reassure them. I negotiated with the bank and worked with them, ensuring I gave regular feedback and financial reports."

Within 12 months the business had made solid progress:

- Salary costs reduced by 45%

- Overall costs reduced by 32%

- Renting out unused grazing facilities, buildings and houses generated £80,000

- Using the farm for film shoots brought in another £48,000

With the changes to the management team, the business needed a new sales manager and Simon's son, Murray, took up the position. He had just finished his masters in oenology and was unaware of the problems until he returned to the farm. When he found out what had happened, he was horrified and wanted to sell up while there was still something left to sell. This affected Simon deeply and for some time he was uncertain whether to keep following the new strategy or simply to sell the business.

Coenie worked hard to convince him, Rozanne and Murray that there was a way forward. "This was the most difficult time; working with the family, giving them my support and sharing knowledge to make them believe in themselves. As we moved into the different stages, gaining momentum and focusing on the critical elements, everyone finally began to see the light."

The difference it made

- The family is now actively involved in the running of the business and, as well as being much stronger and closer as a result, sales have increased by 40% since 2010.

- Murray has brought a renewed passion and modern outlook to the operations of the business and is involved in the winemaking and marketing. They now export 80% of their wine, mainly to the UK and North America, but with growing markets in Hong Kong, Japan, Taiwan and Africa, especially Namibia, Mauritius, Dubai and Tanzania.

- 85 permanent jobs were saved, mainly farm workers. Workers were encouraged to be part of the solution and they played an active role in making the changes, giving them a sense of belonging and real pride in their work. As Coenie says, "The family always treat the workers with respect and dignity. There is love all over the farm and people enjoy working at a successful growing company. Two members of the vineyard team even won Farmworker of the Year Awards in their respective categories this year."

- Simon comments, "Rustenberg has just this year seen a flurry of recognition and awards as a result of the renewed vigour in the business. We were named Most Successful Producer at the Old Mutual Trophy Wine Show, as well as taking home a number of medals across all ranges in a myriad of local and international competitions."

How it made them feel

As Coenie says, the family is hugely grateful for his help. "They have shown their gratitude to me on various occasions. I live about 1600km away from them and always stay over on the farm (in the family house) when I visit them – they insist. When I visit we always talk about the time we worked day and night to save the farm and business and how it has changed to a family managed, profitable and enjoyable business."

And Simon adds, "Today, when we look back it is difficult to believe what we achieved and how quickly we did it. It made us realise that you have to be in touch with your business on a daily basis and be prepared for times of turmoil. There is no greater satisfaction than running a business well and loving what you do! The personal input and support we received from Middel and Partners and especially from Coenie was absolutely invaluable and really helped us to achieve the monumental feat of eradicating bank debts from the farm books and creating a cash flow positive company."

"My accountant helped me change from just a yoga teacher to an entrepreneur"

A one director practice with a team of four, based in Paisley, Scotland that has helped a client:

- Have the confidence to raise prices to a profitable level
- Handle a 'mutiny' of team members so the business could continue
- Keep the business going when the premises were suddenly closed down
- Realise her vision for the future of the business
- Increase her profit... considerably!

The client says, "I've got no idea where I would be now without the support of my accountant."

Background information

Merchant City Yoga (MCY) is a bespoke yoga studio in the centre of Glasgow, run by Judi Farrell since 2012.

The situation at the start

When Judi took over the yoga studio, it had already been running as a business since 2010. The business model was to employ a number of yoga teachers and sub-let space to others to run their own classes. Judi's fee was fixed, no matter how many students were in the classes.

From the start she realised that there were problems in many areas – including her team, the building itself and the landlord. And worse than that, it simply wasn't making enough money so Judi had to do freelance work as a yoga teacher to subsidise MCY.

Although she already had an accountant, when Judi saw that Gloria Murray of Murray Associates was offering a mentoring group to business owners, she knew this was something she wanted to try. "I'd been running my business for about a year when I heard Gloria speak at a networking event. It was actually a pricing discussion and it really made me think. I really liked Gloria and I really liked what she had done with her business as well," Judi says.

How their accountants helped

"We started to work with Judi in September 2013," Gloria says. "First, we conducted a business potential review to ensure she would qualify for the mentoring group. The projections were that she could increase turnover 250%, changing her loss to profit of £19,431. At her first mentoring group session we focused on pricing as a way to kickstart change. Judi came willingly to the meeting, but left with big doubts saying you can't do that in yoga!"

However, Judi knew that she would have to make some changes if she wanted to see a difference in her results and she slowly began to raise her prices. She slightly increased the sub-let rate for teachers and insisted that all classes be priced the same for students, no matter which teacher was running the class. Bookings could be made ahead of time online or by paying the teachers direct on the day.

A few months later she introduced a commission structure based on the number of students attending each class.

And that was when the trouble started.

Gloria explains, "During November / December 2014 two of the teachers who were sub-letting told her they wouldn't follow the new system and they revealed they hadn't increased their prices at all. Their classes were full and Judi had wondered why revenue hadn't gone up. She asked them again to increase their prices and adopt the new commission structure, but they refused.

"She met with us to help her resolve the situation and we suggested there were probably only two options – sack the teachers immediately or give them notice to quit by the end of December so they could find alternative class space. The upshot was they did quit and find alternative space... on the floor below her studio! The landlord was using it as storage space for his bistro and it had fridge freezers in it so you wouldn't think it was suitable for a yoga studio at all. But that's what happened."

Judi already had some issues with the landlord, but this was the last straw. Luckily, her ex-teachers didn't last long in the same building and they soon left to work in another space in the city. Judi began to look for new premises. She was scheduled to spend a month in Australia being tutored by international yoga teachers over January/ February and couldn't find any suitable premises before she left. So she organised classes with the other teachers and left her part-time administrator in charge.

While she was in Australia she had some very bad news – the Fire Brigade had checked the building and found that it didn't meet fire regulations. They closed it down immediately and MCY was shut for business.

"We emailed Judi to try and help," Gloria says, "But we thought that what she probably needed was to hear from the others in the mentoring group. So for the next session we Skyped her in Australia. Everyone was so supportive and she really appreciated being involved and getting their input."

Once back in Glasgow, she found studio space in the function room of a bar-nightclub-casino and started the business again, coincidentally bringing the concept of the pop-up yoga studio to Glasgow!

The team at Murray Associates helped her to find a permanent space and she moved into her current premises in the summer of 2014. When some of the ex-teachers also moved into the city centre with the help of some big investors, Judi was initially very worried. But she found that within a few months she was busier than ever as she began to develop her niche as a high-class bespoke yoga studio.

The difference it made

The mentoring process meant that Gloria was able to have monthly contact with Judi, both within the group and on an individual basis.

"We got more involved with her marketing because she wasn't able to develop the One Page Plan as her bookkeeper was never up to date," Gloria says. "We kept her in touch with her numbers as much as we could and she eventually realised that she needed Murray Associates as her bookkeeper and me as her accountant and mentor."

Judi eventually parted ways with her bookkeeper and Murray Associates took over as her accountant in June 2015.

Starting from a loss in 2013, the business is now seeing steady growth. Even in 2014, when the studio was closed for three months and Judi was using a temporary space, turnover increased by 131%, although profits were very low.

Figures for the year to June 2015 showed a further turnover increase of 131% with profit growth of more than 300%.

Judi is now in a position to recruit quality teachers who buy in to her philosophy of teaching and living yoga. Her students love what she has done and with Gloria's help she has created even more of her own yoga community at MCY.

"Judi is looking at new opportunities and how to make MCY into a teaching centre for yoga teachers in the West of Scotland," Gloria says. "She's organising more yoga retreats and working with us to make them more profitable for her. Her aim is to establish MCY as the leading light for personal and professional yoga development for students and teachers alike. It's been great to see Judi start to realise her potential as a business woman and watch her growing in confidence."

How it made them feel

At the start, Judi was anxious, scared and disillusioned with the team she had inherited at the studio. She was fighting to make a living and a lot was thrown at her in a very short space of time.

In June 2015 she agreed to share her experiences of working with Gloria in a case study. This is just part of what she had to say about being in the mentoring group:

"Clearly there's a lot of practical help, guidance and teaching. That might be bookkeeping and finance and interpreting your accounts. It might be marketing, leadership, staff, whatever it is, there's a lot of real practical advice there, and what's great about being part of the mentoring group is that you get to learn from the other members of your group as well. They all have different experience and in my case, more experience than me, so I learned a lot from them too. Another thing that being part of the group and working with Gloria and Gerry has done for me is completely changing the way that I see myself and the way I view my business.

"At first, I thought I was just a yoga teacher and while I am that and that's massive, I now see myself very much as a business owner and as an entrepreneur even. That's changed my attitude towards myself, towards the work that I do, and also towards my business and the time that I spend on and in my business. The last thing and probably by far the most important thing is just the amount of support that I've had over the course of the programme. As I'm sure you can all sympathise with, my business has had lots of ups and downs over the last two or three years and working with Gloria and Gerry has really helped me ride out some very tough times."

Helping ageing clients to make the most of their last precious days together

A two partner practice with three team members in Illinois, USA, that has helped an ageing client to:

- Deal with all their end of life financial issues
- Make the very most of their precious last days together

"The entire team treat the clients as if they were their grandparents... and seeing them live the values of the firm like this is very special."

Background information

Jody Padar now runs the firm, which had been founded by her father over 40 years ago. It has been transformed under her leadership into one of the most innovative firms in the USA. And she has even written a book, "The Radical CPA", setting out her vision of the new rules for the future ready firm.

However, she has certainly not lost sight of her roots. Her father, now aged 75, is still involved, and a number of their clients have been with them since the very beginning.

"Our clients are part of our extended family," Jody explains. "And, as this section of our client base ages, their needs change. So as part of our commitment to them as members of our extended family, we now help them with all manner of end of life support."

The situation at the start

Frank (his name has been changed for confidentiality reasons) had been a client for 40 years. Sadly, he was then diagnosed with cancer and became very sick.

"Because they were brought up at a time when the men dealt with financial affairs, his wife Jean (name also changed) was like many of our other clients' wives, and didn't know how to deal with the money side of getting old."

As a result, Jean turned to Jody and said, "Frank said you would look after me." And that is exactly what Jody and her team have done for this client, and for many others.

How their accountants helped

They stepped in to take away all the hassle and hard work at an extremely difficult time for the family. This included:

- Pulling together all the details of the couple's assets, and completing the complicated forms and financial statements required for them to apply to move into an assisted living environment

- Relieving Frank of the burden of having to deal with his financial affairs – and making it really easy for Jean to handle them instead, with a lot of help from Jody and her team

- Dealing with the practicalities of passing Frank's estate of over $5 million to Jean when he died, and

- Ensuring that the tax payable on the estate was minimised and dealt with

The difference it made

"We made it seamless. And Jean knew that we were going to make sure that everything was being taken care of," explains Jody. "So she and Frank could concentrate on the far more important job of enjoying their precious last days together, without any financial distractions getting in the way."

How it made them feel

Jody explains, "While we do charge for this kind of end of life support, we genuinely don't make any real money from it. Several people have asked me why. And my answer is always the same: over the many years that they have been clients they have been the ones that paid for me to go through college, paid for my wedding and paid for me to enjoy life. In a very real sense they have given me everything I have. So I really want take care of them through to the end. It is as simple as that."

She adds, "One of the joys for me has been watching my team step up to take care of our clients. And watching them do it in the same way that they would to help their own grandparents. Seeing them live the values of the firm like this way is very special to me."

And their clients really value that kind of caring approach too. In fact, Jean sent Jody and her entire team a hand written thank you note that said, "To the best CPA firm ever. Just to thank you for the help, understanding and kindness you have given me. You are each very special."

"The more money I spend with my accountant the more money I make"

A sole practitioner with a team of seven, based in Leeds, England, who has helped a client:

- Move from 'rock bottom' to 'top of the world'
- Double profits
- Successfully navigate the process of adopting a child
- Become one of the top painting and decorating companies in Yorkshire

As one of the directors puts it, "I can honestly say that working with Northern Accountants has changed the way I look at my business."

Background information

GME is a small commercial painting contractor, serving mainly the construction industry, based in Leeds, but working nationwide. Started by Gavin Esberger and Matthew Edwards in 2007, they began with a van, some brushes and four weeks of confirmed work.

The situation at the start

Gavin and Matthew were at rock bottom. The business was saddled with:

- Low profit margins
- Too many bad clients
- Poor cashflow

Their personal income was limited and they were totally disillusioned with the business. Their day to day commitments meant they had no time to plan so they lacked structure and a vision for the company.

At the time they were working from Matthew's garage, surrounded by stock and attending meetings smelling of paint. They were trying to win the type of contracts they had been used to when they were employed by one of Yorkshire's biggest painting and decorating companies, but it wasn't the business they wanted it to be.

Working long hours in an unsuccessful business added to the stress of family life, and they had reached the stage of not wanting to turn up for work. As a result Gavin and Matthew were considering going back to work for a former employer, although neither of them really wanted to do this having imagined what they could achieve running their own business.

How their accountants helped

In 2013 Gavin and Matthew attended a Business Builder session at Northern Accountants where director Phil Ellerby showed them a piece of profit improvement software called Simple Stuff That Works. It opened their eyes to the potential within their business, and Phil in turn realised that Gavin and Matthew could be very successful business owners.

"They simply lacked clarity of vision and solid structured advice on how to get to their end goal," Phil says now. "Their needs perfectly suited our Numbers programme, an adapted version of the AVN Performance Measurement and Improvement system. Our fee quote came in 33% higher than other accountants and this did cause them some concern. However, our money back guarantee convinced them to invest in our services."

Phil started work straight away. "We began by completing a Personal Balance Sheet for each of them. This was a way of showing them all their assets and liabilities so they could understand how their finances actually stood. It really brought home to them that the business wasn't delivering what they wanted.

"Starting from their Personal Balance Sheet we helped them articulate their personal goals, looking at their incomes, personal wealth, number of hours worked, holidays, work life balance, retirement plans and many other things. And then we mapped their business goals to deliver their personal goals."

One of Gavin's key personal goals was to buy a bigger house so he and his wife Nikki could start a family. But with the low level of earnings he was getting from the business, he hadn't been able to find any additional funding. Phil met his IFA to understand the earnings Gavin and Nikki would need to be able to get a mortgage, and tweaked the business goals to deliver this level for both directors.

Phil continued to work on giving Gavin and Matthew the financial information they needed. "We extended the business goals to create the company's first set of forecasts and corresponding budgets. This was the first time they had a true vision of what the company needed to do to achieve their personal goals."

Phil's forecasts brought to light an issue with cashflow in the summer months when they needed to fund several big projects that were planned. The business had 60 day payment terms for their clients, but 14 and 30 day credit accounts with their contractors and suppliers.

"We worked with the company to secure an invoice finance deal, which is notoriously hard in construction," Phil says. "With this in place by mid-February we set off on the journey to strengthen the company's financial performance and balance sheet value.

"By the summer, the company had built up sufficient reserves and credit lines to trade through the busy periods without the need to use the invoice finance facility."

What's more, savings on interest and charges meant that Gavin and Matthew could buy new cars and vans, which was a huge bonus for them, and a great reflection of their achievement in the year.

How they helped in an even more important way

What happened next was completely unexpected. "Someone tried to blackmail them, threatening to contact their clients and suppliers and spread lies about their conduct. They also threatened to report them to the tax authorities about VAT fraud and tax evasion, which clearly they had not done."

Then the harassment became much more personal.

Gavin and his wife had been trying for a baby for a number of years and had embarked on the adoption process in 2012. In 2014 they moved into a larger house that they had been able to buy since the improvements to the business and were finally in a position to adopt a child. When they were identified as potential adoptive parents of a baby, their dream was on the verge of coming true.

Now the blackmailer threatened to go to the adoption agency, questioning their suitability as adoptive parents. And when the directors refused to cave in, the blackmailer carried out the threat.

As a result, only a week before the adoption was due to be finalised, Gavin and Nikki became the subject of an urgent investigation into complaints made against them. Northern Accountants were asked to an emergency meeting to answer questions on their financial affairs and characters and were able to show that the complaints were completely fabricated. Gavin and Nikki were awarded full custody of baby George (and Phil was even asked to be his godfather).

Having dealt with that emergency, Phil helped Gavin and Matthew develop a One Page Business Plan to record and measure their key performance numbers monthly. He also began to attend the monthly board meetings and they worked together on the ideal client profile for the business. During this process it became clear that they needed to move away from the construction industry where most of their existing clients were based and into new markets, in particular repaints in the housing, retail and commercial sectors. This would mean higher margins, better payment terms and less exposure to application disputes.

To succeed in these new areas, the business needed to update their brand. Once again, Phil and his team stepped in. "We helped them create a strategic marketing plan through our own marketing company. It has seen the business develop a new website, improve their brand consistency, develop strong marketing collateral and enhance their social media presence."

In early 2015 the directors were also able to change their roles so that Matthew could run the operations side of the business while Gavin moved to business development.

The difference it made

Between 2012 and 2014 the business:

- Increased turnover by 99%
- Increased gross profit by 130%
- Increased net profit by 81%
- Increased post tax profits by 100%

"They have grown from a small company to a medium sized company," Phil says, "and the perception in the market is that they are one of the big boys. They are equal in status to companies they once worked for and are on the road to being recognised as one of the top three painting and decorating companies in Yorkshire."

In addition:

- Their cash flow is much improved, their processes work and are adhered to and they have a much better idea of the clients they want.

- They know which jobs to go for rather than rushing in for jobs they couldn't sustain.

- They plan resources and material more efficiently with a process in place to cost each job.

- Good processes and systems now cover all departments and every new system is written down in an 'Idiot's Guide'.

- The future is much clearer and the directors know exactly where they want to go and what the business will do for them in retirement, for the benefit of them, their employees and their families.

- The existing work force is still employed and has doubled in size.

- The team enjoy a much better remuneration/benefits package, with more holidays.

- Both families enjoy quality time and the extra income.

As Gavin says, "I now know where every penny of my money goes to in the business."

How it made them feel

Gavin and Matthew themselves suggested to Phil that he submit their case story for this book – a testament to the life-changing impact he has had on their business and on their lives.

"They are delighted with the progress the company has made and are now pressing even harder for further success, setting even higher targets than before," Phil comments. "What's more, they have generated over £50,000 of additional fees for us through introductions to their contacts. For example, Gavin introduced us to his brother in law, a very shrewd business man. After meeting him we went on to sign up four other businesses operating in the buildings he owns, bringing in fees in excess of £15,000 per annum."

The fees that GME pay to Northern Accountants have doubled to £12,000 per annum, not something that fazes either of the directors. As Gavin recently said, "The more money I spend with you, Phil, the more money I make."

Creating financial peace of mind for a client with cancer

Numbers UK is a 9 person practice based in Plymouth, England that has helped a client:

- Cope with life-threatening cancer
- Pay for expensive medical treatment
- Create financial peace of mind for his family
- Save 15 jobs

"We are most proud that we were able to help this client and his family through their darkest hour," says the firm's principal.

Background information

The client (who must remain anonymous for reasons of confidentiality) owns a successful business based in the South West of England.

At its height, the company employed 35 people and generated sales of £2.5m. But then the business suffered a devastating triple blow: the client was diagnosed with life-threatening cancer, a key team member left under a cloud, and there was a major downturn in their market due to the recession.

The situation at the start

Steven Carey, the firm's principal, explains, "Our client was facing an uncertain future and was unsure of the best way to proceed. He had the option of selling his business, with the risk that local jobs would be lost. He could try to rebuild his team and sales while battling with cancer. Or he could find someone to succeed him as managing director.

"Unfortunately, the initial candidate he identified as the new managing director tried to mount a coup, and left the business when it failed. That left our client with no clear succession plan, and a significant risk of other key employees following the ring leader out of the company."

138

How their accountants helped

Steven Carey and his team at Numbers UK helped by:

- **Implementing a share ownership scheme** – which allowed a key team member to take an equity stake in the business, and incentivised him to take on the role of interim managing director, despite his initial extreme unwillingness to take on the job.

- **Establishing a more rigorous management information reporting system** – so the business owner could concentrate on his cancer treatment without losing touch with his company's performance.

- **Regularly recalculating his family's retirement income requirements** – demonstrating how this could be delivered whether the company continued or was sold off, and reassuring him that his very expensive cancer treatment could be paid for.

- **Developing a whole team business ownership model** – working with the interim managing director to create and incentivise a new leadership team that covers all the normal Board responsibilities, but does not have a named individual as managing director.

The difference it made

"At the start," Steven explains, "the client's stress levels were very high, and he was starting to make poor decisions. As a result, his team members (and us as his accountants) were sometimes subjected to unreasonable requests and outbursts.

"In providing a knowledgeable sounding board, we allowed the client to vent his frustrations, and provide clarity to his thinking. More importantly, we were able to a put an end to his fears about the affordability of his cancer treatment.

"As a result, he now sees the future as much less stressful, and is delighted that a suitable management team is being created to succeed him. So he is able to take much more of a back seat role, and concentrate on getting well."

In addition, Steven believes that this approach has also saved about 15 local jobs, "because about half of the employees would have been made redundant had the company been sold." Instead, those same employees are now being offered the chance to own shares in the company, securing their financial future and potentially helping them to create wealth for their families.

How it made them feel

Initially, the client was extremely anxious, and with good reason. In addition to the normal stresses of running a business, his industry was hit really hard by the recession, his cashflow concerns were magnified by the need to pay for his cancer treatment, and he was really worried about leaving his widow with a debt legacy.

"We are still part way through the project," says Steven. "But the client has now achieved real clarity and peace, because he no longer needs to worry about the finances of his business or his family. So if I had to sum up his feelings in one word, he is 'relieved.'

"As a team we are proud of the fact that we have been trusted to help deliver the company's new ownership model. We are proud that we 'stepped forward' and went on risk for our fees, when so many others would have sought to limit their involvement and protect themselves from a potential bad debt. We are proud that we helped to save so many local jobs. And we are most proud that we were able to help this client and his family through their darkest hour."

As a footnote, Steven and his team have also earned thousands of pounds in fees by supporting their client in these ways. So doing the right thing paid off commercially too!

How perseverance transformed the fortunes of a struggling business

A two director practice with a team of 15 in Eastbourne, England that helped a client to:

- Avoid liquidation
- Build a reputation for quality that allows it to win profitable work
- Increase profits to £650,000

"We make a difference by giving him 'the right information – to make the right decisions – at the right time'. And in return we can charge higher fees."

Background information

The client is an outside contracting business in the South of England.

The situation at the start

Mike Ogilvie of OBC explains, "The client originally came to OBC because his sales were growing, but profits weren't, and he was getting very little advice from his accountants.

"He had an ex-bank manager as financial controller, but the management figures he produced lacked any credibility, and consequently the bank refused to support him. I offered advice, but there was a reluctance to allow us to get too involved because of the potential cost, and the fact that the ex-bank manager felt threatened by us. In the end, though, things got so bad that they called me in an emergency to see if I could help save the business."

How their accountants helped

To buy the business time, and prevent the creditors taking precipitative action that would have forced it into liquidation, Mike brought in an insolvency specialist and they put it into a Corporate Voluntary

Arrangement (CVA). This made it possible for Mike and his team to:

- Develop an action plan to restore profitability

- Put in place more robust management information systems, once the ex-bank manager had left

- Hold quarterly meetings with the business to review the results and fine tune the action plan

- Negotiate an agreement where their main creditor would accept slightly less than 50% of what was owed, paid over a three year period

"As a result, after three years they had successfully traded through the CVA, making a steady though not spectacular profit. However, six months later some of the old ways had slipped back in, and I was horrified to find he was suddenly making a loss of £100k."

Mike quickly identified the cause: "He used to employ a large permanent workforce. Not only was this a very expensive fixed cost, but because they didn't do a very good job, rework costs were also decimating his margins.

"This was one of the first things we had changed during the CVA, paying sub contracted teams per contract rather than per day. And although they effectively earned more per day than the previous employees, they only got paid when the business needed them and their contracts were completed satisfactorily. As a result, fixed costs were reduced, jobs were done a lot more efficiently, rework costs were slashed, and consequently they had started to become consistently profitable."

Despite these disciplines having served him well during the hard times, once things improved the client "became too bullish (and perhaps even complacent)", and started employing more permanent team members again. Which, of course, had an immediately negative effect on costs, efficiency and profitability.

"Fortunately, we were able to intervene quickly and get things back on track. And I think it was at this point that he first fully understood the value of the discipline, focus and independent perspective we provide. So he now insists on getting a full management accounting, mentoring and advisory service from us.

"As part of that we have changed his accounting system from Sage to Xero and introduced the Workflow Max add-on to accurately measure and monitor the performance and profitability of every contract."

The difference it made

When Mike was appointed as their accountant, the business was facing extinction. Last year, profits exceeded £500,000, this year they are likely to be more than £650,000. "Better still, he now seems well on his way to £1 million profit in the year ahead, which would make a very lucrative exit possible for him."

Obviously not all of this success is down to Mike and his team. But they have undoubtedly played a key role in it, "because the staffing arrangements we recommended meant that work is done to a much higher standard, they now have a reputation for quality that results in them being asked to quote for profitable work rather than having to chase work at low prices and margins."

How it made them feel

"The client is so grateful that we helped him save his business when all looked lost, and is really excited at how successful and profitable it has become," explains Mike.

"The really satisfying thing for us is that he now trusts us unquestioningly, sees us as an integral part of his team and involves us in all the important issues. We make a difference by giving him 'the right information – to make the right decisions – at the right time'. And in return we can charge him higher fees, making it a win-win all round.

"For me it's a great example of the power of persevering. We persevered even when the client wasn't very receptive. And we helped him to persevere however bad things got. As a result he now has a really strong business, and we have a really good client."

Helping a burned out client get his work-life balance back under control

Sole practitioner in Barcelona, Spain who has helped a client to:

- No longer be dependent on its owner
- No longer force the owner to get by on four hours sleep a night
- Improve the stress levels and happiness of everyone in his business
- Provide invaluable support for disabled people
- Meet monthly to focus on the key financial and strategic issues

"The most important thing to me is that, one business at a time, as accountants we really can change the world for our clients, their teams and the customers they serve," says the practitioner.

Background information

Founded in 2011, the client is a small business in Barcelona, Spain that specialises in helping disabled people.

The situation at the start

In May 2014, before they were his clients, Oriol Lopez received an email saying, "We are thinking about changing our business advisers because we don't feel we are currently getting the strategic, financial and tax input that we need to take the business forward."

"When I met the business owner it was obvious that he really wanted to grow his business so that he could help more disadvantaged people," Oriol said. "So his vision was clear, and the business was profitable. But the problem was that he was so involved in the administrative side of things that he wasn't able to focus on the strategic and growth issues."

How their accountants helped

By digging deeper Oriol was able to identify three key areas to focus on:

Better management information – Financial controls were weak, and they were relying on a complicated collection of spreadsheets. As a result they couldn't make fully informed strategic or financial decisions, they regularly ran out of cash despite being profitable, and it was often impossible for the business owner to pay himself a salary.

"Better controls, better accounting and better cash flow forecasting were part of the solution. But probably the most useful thing we did was to help them create a One Page Plan. This brings all the key performance indicators for the business together on a single A4 page. And it's this that we focus on in our regular monthly strategic meetings with them. In fact, it is central to my new role as their strategic advisor.

"In fact, because it measures financial and non-financial KPI's, it is used by everyone in the business, not just by financially oriented people. For example, by measuring the number of meetings with prospects and clients, website leads generated and referrals received, it helps everyone involved in sales get better results by making better decisions based on better information."

Better tax planning – "When we started with them their tax planning was non-existent, so they were paying excessive tax unnecessarily," explained Oriol. "So we proactively carried out a comprehensive review looking for every tax benefit that they could take advantage of, no matter how small the saving was."

Better use of talent – "People were doing the wrong jobs in the business. This was most obvious with the owner, because the business and everyone in it were completely dependent on him, so he was forced to work ridiculously long hours and get by on four hours sleep a night. And inevitably this prevented him from dedicating time to strategy. Many of the other team members were also stressed and unhappy because they didn't really know how to do things, felt powerless because they were frequently completely reliant on the owner to sort things out, and as a result were inefficient, unproductive and kept making mistakes."

Oriol helped them tackle these issues by:

*   **Systemising the business** – This involved creating and implementing standard forms, templates and processes. Not only did this make it easier and quicker for everybody to do their jobs, more consistently and with fewer mistakes. But it also made it much easier for the owner to delegate tasks to his team, and for them to take over those tasks with much less stress.

- **Redistributing tasks** – The new systems-based approach also made it possible for work to be allocated to people based on their willingness and enthusiasm to do it. And as a result people became much happier with their roles, and much more productive in them.
- **Interruption management** – This involved showing the team how to reduce and manage interruptions better.

The difference it made

As Oriol explains "We only started working with them in 2014, so this is still very much work in progress. But already the impact has been dramatic." For example:

- They are getting better results because they are making better and more informed decisions
- Cashflow pressures have been greatly reduced – and can now be predicted and managed
- Preventing unexpected cashflow crises has made the business safer and more secure
- For the first time in their history they have generated enough cash to distribute some of the profits back to the owner
- They have also generated enough cash to invest in their growth by hiring a two person sales and marketing team (creating two new jobs in the process) and buying bigger and better located premises to operate from
- Their ordinary tax burden has been reduced by more than 10%, and they bought the new premises in a very tax efficient way

"Most importantly of all, the business now works more smoothly than ever before, with far fewer stressful interruptions and costly mistakes. And the business owner now works sensible hours and has all the time he needs to focus on strategy and management."

How it made them feel

Oriol explained, "When we started working together our client was desperately worried and stressed because of the huge cash flow pressure and the fact that he didn't really know what was going on or how to move forward. And he was completely burned out because everything was on his shoulders and he wasn't able to delegate.

"Every business has difficult moments. But those moments are now the exception for him, and he has a much better professional and personal life. He is able to work on the strategy and plan growth without getting sucked into all the operational details. And that brings him great joy and motivation, because by growing the business he is able to pursue his passion for helping even more disadvantaged people. Alongside all of that, he now has much more time for himself and his family (and to sleep), and is now able to take holidays without once worrying about the business.

"In fact, the changes have had a really positive effect on everybody in the business: they are now all less stressed, more engaged and happier than ever."

But as Oriol makes clear, the impact doesn't end there: "The most important thing to me is that in all these small ways, one business at a time, as accountants we really can change the world for our clients, their teams and the customers they serve. On top of which, the €10,000 this particular client invested in our fees is very nice too!"

Making a real difference globally and locally

Owadally & King is a two partner practice in Croydon, England that is:

- Making life better for those living in poor and underprivileged parts of the world
- Helping budding local entrepreneurs from disadvantaged backgrounds become successful
- Supporting young people launch their careers

"I was getting stale... but this has changed my life"

That's how Simon Maddox described the impact that becoming "socially responsible" has had on him and his practice. And it's making a real difference commercially too.

Simon is one of two partners at Owadally & King ('O&K'), a practice with a total team of 17 people and a strong focus on tax. A few years ago he wrote down his goal as being to retire to the Yorkshire Dales by 2016.

Now he is not so sure, as he is enjoying practice more than ever before.

What changed?

In late 2011 Simon heard about the initial plans for the Accountants Changing The World movement (www.accountantschangingtheworld. com), and they resonated with his values as a man of faith. So much so, in fact, that it started him on a journey that has resulted in O&K making a profound difference:

- Globally to the lives of those living in poor and underprivileged parts of the world

- Locally to budding entrepreneurs from disadvantaged backgrounds

- And also to the future of the local community, by helping its young people launch their careers

It has also helped O&K in striving to achieve a balance between assisting wealthy clients through tax planning and other accountancy related services, as well as helping those less fortunate.

International impact

Inspired by the way Accountants Changing The World works with the B1G1 Business For Good movement (www.b1g1.com), Simon showed the global charity International Needs (www.ineeds.org.uk) how it could enable people and businesses to give to the projects the charity supports.

And, leading by example, O&K now does exactly that through International Needs by automatically:

- Giving life-saving vaccinations every time it completes an annual return for a client

- Giving life-enhancing books to third world schools every time it finalises a set of accounts

- And giving an African family a sustainable source of food and an income, in the form of chickens, every time it wins a new client

But that is only the start.

Local impact on budding entrepreneurs

"We wanted to make a real difference locally too," explained Simon. "So when an innovative Community Interest Company ('CIC') came to us, having been let down by another firm, not only did we get to solve their accountancy issue within 24 hours, but we also got involved in their community work."

Enterprise Cube CIC (www.enterprisecube.org) runs business start-up training courses for the residents of housing associations. The courses are free to delegates, because they are paid for by the housing associations, and give their tenants (many of whom are from very disadvantaged backgrounds) the skills, knowledge and confidence they need to set up their own businesses.

"Housing associations are so keen to get involved, that it is difficult keeping up with demand," says Simon. "But it is really worth it, because the calibre and potential of some of the businesses we have helped to start is amazing. For example, one of the businesses I now mentor is a hat maker, and one of her hats was recently seen on the BBC Television's Graham Norton show being worn by the singer Paloma Faith."

O&K help out in six main ways:

1. **Mentoring** – Currently Simon is mentoring two fledgling entrepreneurs who have been through Enterprise Cube's training programme.

2. **Lecturing** – Providing some of the basic book-keeping and understanding accounts elements of the training programme.

3. **Drop in centre** – On the first Friday of every month Simon takes his laptop and works remotely from Enterprise Cube's offices. And every single entrepreneur who has been through the training programme knows that they can drop in on those days without an appointment and get instant free help from him.

4. **Business Jam events** – Once a month Enterprise Cube invites experts from three different marketing firms, three law firms and three HR firms to sit in a room together for an evening and provide free advice to anybody who wants it. "They used to invite three accountancy firms as well. But now they tend to ask us to provide three members of staff, because we work really hard to pitch our advice at the right level – i.e. not so simple as to be condescending, but not so complex as to be off-putting."

5. **Dragons Den style panels, but with a difference** – The difference is that the panel is designed to be supportive, and every business that presents to the panel leaves with either some funding, some constructive advice or even, in some cases, a local government / housing association contract, since the leaders of the Council and Housing Association are also on the panel!

6. **Strategic advice to the Community Interest Company itself** – As trusted and committed partners, O&K are now helping the CIC to develop its strategy for growth so that it can meet the huge demand for its services.

Local impact on young people

"We have also now started working with The Hive Croydon, initially as sponsors. They deliver an employability skills programme for young people. And that is also really exciting as it helps children aged 5-19, especially those from disadvantaged backgrounds, to get an even better education that lays the foundation for a successful life and career."

Impact on the practice

Simon was really keen to stress that "we categorically aren't doing this for the money, and we never try to sell any of our services to any of the entrepreneurs we help.

"But the really interesting thing is that, once people get to trust us, they tend to take the initiative in asking us to become their accountants on commercial terms. It's a slow burn, but it really does work that way."

In fact, the benefits of giving in the way they do include:

- The three charities/CICs they work most closely with have all appointed O&K as their accountants

- As have some of the businesses they have helped. "Interestingly, the most recent drop-in centre day resulted in us picking up three new clients. Two at £250 each, and one at £1,500. So the slow burn is really beginning to spiral now."

- And the O&K team are energised. "I have been amazed at how quickly and fully the team have taken to it. They now really understand and are excited by the fact that business is not all about take, take, take. That in turn is improving service levels, productivity and job satisfaction across the firm."

But perhaps the greatest benefit of all is what lies behind Simon's assertion that "this has changed my life."

"If I'm honest, I was getting a bit stale. But now I really look forward to coming to work. It's so fulfilling knowing that we are part of something that is making a real difference.

"And we're not just helping to solve 'easy' problems, either. We are helping to solve some of society's most intractable problems, because some of the people helped have been former gang members, drug addicts or homeless.

"Who would have thought that as accountants we can make a difference in those sorts of areas? But I can tell you we can. And we are. In fact, it's now why I get up in the morning."

Far-sighted support has changed the way this business thinks and acts

A single director practice with a team of 14 based in Whitstable, Kent, UK, that has helped its client:

- Break forever the stereotype of a typical double glazing firm
- Future-proof a rapidly expanding business at risk of growing too fast
- Gain a sense of direction and purpose for the business
- Understand the business far better so they can make decisions with confidence

As the client says, "The impact has been profound in every single area of the business; this goes way beyond mere financial reporting."

Background information

P&P Windows is a family-run trade supplier and installer of quality windows, doors, conservatories and porches in Kent and the surrounding areas. They have been trading for around four years and have a showroom and office based in Ramsgate Kent, with five installation teams and a trade counter. P&P have gone through significant growth in recent years and turnover is in excess of £2m per annum.

The situation at the start

Within P&P, the experience and knowledge of the windows and door industry is exceptional and they are committed to delighting their customers and breaking the stereotype of a typical double glazing business. However, P&P recognised that they had outgrown their current structure and processes and were in need of additional business support if they were to continue to be successful in future. This was even more crucial as they were in the process of setting up a sister company and wanted this to have a firm foundation right from the start.

How their accountants helped

PH Accountancy conducted an end-to-end review of the business, identifying which areas needed support. They then worked together with the business owners to put strong processes and practices in place.

The key improvements were:

- **Strategy planning** – They worked with the business to introduce a structured strategy including creating a mission statement and vision, establishing business values and an annual balanced scorecard/objectives.

- **Customer satisfaction programme** – They developed a new customer satisfaction survey, created a measurement matrix, reporting tool and management review so the business owners understood their customers much better than before.

- **Employee satisfaction programme** – They created an annual employee satisfaction survey, analysed the initial set of data and developed an action plan so they could respond to their employees and increase team happiness.

- **Cash management** – They looked into the key cash processes until they had a thorough understanding of how they worked then discussed improvement opportunities with the business owners. They created a 'Cash Management Improvement Plan' to include cash reporting, cash forecasting, improved banking management and payment timings.

- **Team support** – They supported the business owners in numerous staffing matters and also helped with recruitment of new team members.

- **Process support** – They reviewed the business processes and identified efficiency opportunities and process failures to increase overall effectiveness.

- **Business performance measurement** – They created a weekly sales reporting analysis tool to include: product analysis, average sales value, volume analysis, forecasting, comparison to target and prior year.

- **New showroom** – When the business opened a new showroom, they provided project support in terms of planning and costing the move so it went as smoothly as possible.

- **Business coach** – When one of the business owners stepped away to set up a new business, they provided additional business support to the remaining business owner whenever necessary.

- **Customer communication** – They helped the business owner with key client communications, particularly in cases of customer disputes.
- **General business support** – At the regular meetings they had together, the business owner was able to gain feedback and suggestions on day-to-day issues and ideas from an outsider's perspective.

The difference it made

With the insights the business owners now have, they've gained the confidence to make decisions on new clients, new products and new staff. In the last 18 months a new sales manager, an install manager and a factory junior have been taken on. Other benefits include:

- They have a strong sense of business direction and planning
- The strong processes, practices and governance that have been put in place have future-proofed business growth
- They have an avenue to discuss and resolve day-to-day issues
- They now have full insight into how their business works, as well as how their customers and employees are thinking

Showing the trust that P&P have in PH Accountancy, they have now asked them to act in a similar capacity for their sister company, Rhino Aluminium Ltd.

As the business owners commented, "The insight, focus and support that PH Accountancy provides has been invaluable, and we see them as an integral part of our success."

How it made them feel

Before the additional support from PH Accountancy, the business owners were concerned for the future. Despite the fact that the business was performing well, they were worried that it was growing too fast, too soon, and that the existing structure wasn't strong enough to take them to the next level. They were also worried that they were not adequately measuring their business, which was crucial if they were to continue to grow.

As the business owners say, "We are now so much more self-aware as a business, with a much better structure in place and we're in a good position to successfully develop our plans for the future."

Iain Hamnett of PH Accountancy is particularly proud that the support they provided has built a really strong relationship between both businesses. "This level of business advice would mean nothing if P&P were not receptive to change. They recognised the advice was valuable, agreed to implement the changes and vitally, they recognised that they needed to change to progress."

Using cloud based automation tools to make a business more efficient and profitable

Pillow May is a one director firm with a team of five (all working mums), based in Wiltshire, England, that has helped a client:

- Increase sales volume at the same time as increasing prices by 10-25%
- Comfortably beat an ambitious growth target of 33%
- Put systems in place so the business can run without her

"I wanted to make my family proud of me. And thanks to my accountant, they really are," says the client.

Background information

Savage Beauty is a high-end beauty salon offering treatments and a retail space for clients wanting expert personalised skincare advice. It is based in the Wiltshire town of Devizes and was opened by owner Emma Savage in 2011.

The situation at the start

Emma comes from a family of entrepreneurs and, having identified the need for this type of salon in Devizes, was keen to start her own business.

Aged just 21, she found a property which offered her the space she needed and, with financial help from her family and a legacy from her late father, took on a 10 year lease. Without previous experience of running a business, it was a big gamble.

The salon proved very popular and the client list expanded rapidly. Emma took on additional therapists but found it harder and harder to pay the rent each month. Feeling increasingly stressed, she had to inject her personal money into the business to keep it afloat.

When her finances still didn't improve, she cut back on her team, but this meant that the retail shop was closed when they were busy with treatments. Takings went down even further as a result.

She didn't know what to do for the best and was seriously considering giving up and closing the salon.

How their accountants helped

Emma realised that she needed proper advice and turned to Wiltshire Business Support (an advice service for small businesses) for help. They recommended she speak to Jessica Pillow of Pillow May. Although Emma had limited funds available, she was able to get grant funding of 50% as Jessica is accredited through the Growth Voucher scheme,

"Together, we went through Emma's original aims for the business and identified which things weren't working," Jessica says. "We put together a sketch budget to work out the number of treatments required per week to achieve break-even point and to ensure that the salon was actually viable. This was information she simply hadn't had before."

Jessica then developed an action plan for Emma:

- Increase margins through a 10% price increase on treatments by the assistant therapist and a 25% price increase for Emma (as senior therapist).

- Set up Receipt Bank, a cloud based tool for scanning and automatically processing purchase invoices and receipts – to save time on data entry for accounts and tax purposes, and to store business records more efficiently

- Switch to Timely, a cloud-based system that allows clients to book their own appointment slots, reduces no shows by automatically sending reminders, and automatically creates sales invoices once the appointment has happened. It also acts as a contact management system that can drive marketing campaigns. Because Timely saved Emma's team a lot of time on administrative tasks, it gave them much more time to make sales by serving in the shop and doing treatments.

- Integrate Timely and Receipt Bank with Xero, so that large parts of the sales and purchasing functions were automated, and comprehensive management information could be produced at the push of a button.

And it was all to be completed within three weeks!

Pillow May offered support throughout the process, both for the software and as a personal mentor for Emma. All the changes were made by the beginning of November, to capitalise on the busy pre-Christmas period.

As a result of the new systems, Emma had a lot of key information available for the first time:

- She could see which treatments were popular and which were less so, making it easy to identify trends and take early action to avoid problems.

- She had better knowledge of her clients, as she had all their contact details at her fingertips and knew who her best customers were.

- She had full stock reports, so it was easier to reduce inventory levels by adopting a just in time purchasing strategy – which was a big boost to her cashflow.

- She could see in advance when the salon would be busy – or quiet – so was able to better manage her team costs.

The difference it made

Emma had her best Christmas ever, with increased bookings for treatments at higher prices. She was also able to reduce her stock, and started January with money in the bank.

A planned hospital procedure in January took Emma away from the business for a month, but with the new systems in place, her assistant kept the business running.

Jessica comments, "Emma offered 25% discount on any bookings while she was away, so her assistant would stay busy. It was also a way of encouraging her own clients to give her assistant a try with their treatments so Emma could be freed up in the future to work 'on' the business. And in fact, sales figures for the month were better than the previous January."

When Emma returned, she and Jessica put together a budget with the ambitious target of a 33% month by month increase in sales from the previous year. This would allow her to take a proper director's salary each month as well as a small dividend for the year. Remarkably, by the end of July, the business was already operating at 10% over budget for the year to date.

"The business plan has given Emma focus and the ability to make decisions confidently on the future of her business," Jessica says. "She feels far more in control. The level of stress and worry has greatly reduced and a number of long-time clients have commented on how 'the old Emma' is back.

"Our regular meetings ensure she is always aware of her financial figures and that keeps her focused on where the business is going. It's an ideal opportunity for her to bounce ideas around and review her business plan."

Emma is planning to hire extra team members later this year and her partner has now become a director, allowing them to plan for their future together as well as for the business. Her employees also have a better understanding of the business and appreciate the more relaxed and efficient working environment that the new software and systems have created.

How it made them feel

From the start Emma knew she had a good business idea, but until she met Jessica she didn't have the guidance she needed to make it work and was becoming increasingly frustrated.

"I wanted to make my own decisions and make my family proud," Emma says now. "But when I asked for advice before, I felt that no one took me seriously because I was such a young business woman. Having Jessica is like having a business partner who I can bounce ideas off at any time. She explains all the financial data and reasoning behind her recommendations, but I am still in control of my decisions."

Helping a client take control and create a successful business

Powerful Accounting is a seven person firm based in Connecticut, USA, that has helped a client:

- No longer feel like a "moron"
- Build a $1 million business
- Take control of the financials
- Turn their employees into intrapreneurs and entrepreneurs

"I am really proud that she feels we have played a key part in her success," says the firm's owner.

Important note

Unlike most of the other chapters in this book, the story below has not been written by the authors. Instead, every single word of it was written in ready-to-publish form by the accountant herself, Dawn W. Brolin, CPA of Powerful Accounting.

Background information

Sherree Goldstein worked in the drug and alcohol field for about 12 years, but she dreamed of opening a small coffee shop. She wanted to offer patrons a delectable menu made from fresh, organic, seasonal and local foods. The quality and tastiness of the ingredients were vitally important, as was creating a friendly neighbourhood café that would bring the community together.

In 2003, Sherree and her business partner brought Square Café to the popular Regent Square area of Pittsburgh, PA. They hired eight staff members and by the end of the second week had 21. Sherree didn't know it at the time, but she was about to embark on a journey into the restaurant industry that would change her life in more ways than one.

Sherree and her business partner parted ways after two years and she became the sole owner of Square Café. This was a smart decision. By 2005, Square Café reached $435,000 in sales. In 2006, sales were $800,000. This was due to a combination of local advertising and marketing and, crucially, Sherree's input. She turned the staff around and made sure the restaurant was running smoothly.

Her dream of opening a little coffee shop had turned into a much larger endeavour. This led to questions about the restaurant's financials and, unbeknownst to Sherree, the café's finances weren't that great.

It was time for her to take control of the business and start working ON it in addition to working IN it.

The situation at the start

I met Sherree at the 2011 Spark and Hustle conference in Pittsburgh, PA. She stated that she was looking for an accountant. So I shouted, "I am an accountant!" And we spoke for some time, and decided that I would fly out to Pittsburgh to see her café and the day-to-day business.

Holy moly! The food and service at Square Café is incredible.

However, even though the business experienced major growth – sales had tripled – the business was suffering 'financially' for many reasons:

- The previous accountant wasn't familiar with the restaurant industry.

- Sherree didn't know how much waste Square Café had.

- Square Café had debt.

- She received compiled financial statements every month. But they weren't in that great of shape and didn't have any connection to Square Café's tax returns.

- The accountant didn't review Square Café's financial statements with her, and didn't give her any input along the lines of, "This is where you stand. And this is what last month looked like."

- Financial analysis wasn't being done at a deep level. For example, Sherree had no idea what the omelettes cost when they were served to customers. They may have cost $2.27. But she didn't know for sure.

- Sherree files as an S-Corp and was not reaping the benefits of her labours because she didn't know what her numbers were.

Needless to say, the previous accountant didn't provide her with any growth advice either.

So her back was against the wall. She was frustrated, aggravated, and felt like a moron. Sherree was doing her best, but she's not an accountant.

After our first meeting, she hired us and has become the perfect client because she understands that she's investing in her business. And most importantly, she is willing to do what it takes and is open to learning.

How their accountants helped

Sherree needed to be in control and engaged in Square Café. We initially met bi-weekly, so my Powerful Accounting team and I could get our hands on Square Café's financials and dig into them. I made it clear that it was important for Sherree's accounting records to be on site, so she could review them with or without the Powerful Accounting team. This meant giving her access to the world of Intuit programs such as QuickBooks and Full Service Payroll.

Payroll was somewhat of a mess because it wasn't broken out properly. You couldn't tell if someone was a manager, direct service or worked in the front or back of the house. To correct this, Intuit Full Service Payroll was implemented and we taught Sherree how to use it. Since Square Café is an S-Corp, Sherree personally receives a paycheck and W2 (because she is treated as an employee). So now she processes the payroll, can see exactly what it is every week, and is firmly in control of this hugely important element of her costs.

Thanks to the technology we introduced, we were also able to clean up, and properly set up, the rest of her financials. For example, bank reconciliations are now much easier to perform and are reconciled every week (quarterly is far too late). This allows us to catch any errors and correct them immediately. It also makes it possible to identify and deal with bounced checks and other financial emergencies sooner rather than later.

We have also taught her that analysis is imperative. For example, we analyse advertising to see how much Sherree spends and what she gets from it. And I'll say to her things like, "Tell me what you got for the $4,000 you spent. Let's look at your plate count. Has it gone up? What does your seat count look like? Are your staff asking customers how they heard about Square Café?"

Gathering data like that is helping Sherree to make better decisions for her business now and in the future.

The difference it made

Because of what she has learned from us, Sherree is now also teaching her employees the importance of intrapreneurship and entrepreneurship. As a result, when customers walk into the restaurant, the staff know that how they greet customers, and everything else they do, can make or break Square Café, their performance reviews and their bonuses. So they treat Square Café as if it was their business, and this translates to an increase in sales and positive attitudes.

As a result Square Cafe is now a million-dollar business, employs 30-40 people, and in 2015 Sherree earned more than at any time in the previous 3 years. Because of this, she's been able to make sure her staff are properly paid too. She now also pays quarterly performance bonuses and provides employees with health, vision, dental and life insurance.

At one of our regular monthly meetings to review the numbers, she said to me, "Brolin, I don't know what is going on. But I think I can give myself a bonus for August 2015." I thought she had lost her mind! However, we looked at the numbers and profitability was up $25,000 when compared to August 2014. So, for the first time in ages, she was able to pay herself a very big bonus.

But it is not just Sherree and her team who are benefitting.

Because she has a big heart, she also enrolls 16-year-olds onto a summer work program, helping them to build their personal and professional skills, and teaching them to be intrapreneurial and entrepreneurial alongside the rest of the team. The experience is invaluable to them.

She also partners with many local nonprofits on fundraisers, special events, and promotions. And even allows local artists to use Square Cafe as a gallery to showcase their work.

How it made them feel

Sherree has now become a pro at using QuickBooks, taking control of Square Café's financials and understanding what the business means. In fact, recently she said to me "I've been able to cut the roof out and look into my business. I'm saving money and learned how to work on my business. It's great!"

She now also has a proper work/life balance. She's been able to take more vacations than in previous years and give her mom a set amount each month. She's saving money for retirement (if she ever retires). And she has more confidence when it comes to working ON and running Square Café.

Better still, she no longer thinks of herself of a moron and her frustration has gone.

Sherree is a savvy restaurant owner who understands that not only is she investing in her future, but the future of her employees and the community she serves. And I am really proud that she feels we have played a key part in her success.

Improving 91,819 lives by inspiring a client to become a "Business For Good"

RJS Accounting, a single partner firm with 7 team members in Queensland, Australia, helped a client:

- Grow its retail business by 65% in two and a half years
- Transform itself by gaining a profound new sense of purpose
- Make life better for 91,819 people in need

The firm's owner says, "We believe that people with passion can change the world for the better."

Background information

Kobomo is an independent women and children's boutique based in Noosaville, Queensland. Owned and run by Karen Ormerod, it designs its own range of clothing and ethically manufactures it in a home-based business in Thailand.

RJS accounting, which is run by Kylie Anderson, is based a few miles down the road in Tewantin. Its website proudly proclaims: "Some accountants crunch numbers... we change lives! We believe that people with passion can change the world for the better. So our mission is to help our clients achieve more than they thought possible, and have fun doing it!"

The situation at the start

While Kobomo had always been a good business, it relied on Excel spreadsheets and didn't have a proper management information system. As a result its margins weren't right, and it was underperforming.

How their accountants helped

Since being appointed two and a half years ago RJS has:

- Moved it from its cumbersome Excel spreadsheets to Xero
- Produced meaningful and useful management information
- Put in place integrated point of sale and stock systems
- Reviewed its prices, costs and margins
- Acted as a sounding board for ideas and issues
- Met with the team monthly as part of the breakfast group the practice runs to help local business leaders and professionals work together to share insights and solve their respective problems.

The difference it made

Kobomo's turnover has increased by 65% in the two and a half years it has worked with Kylie and her RJS team. "We don't believe for one moment that we deserve all the credit," explains Kylie, "but they are adamant that their growth is all down to us."

Perhaps more importantly, however, RJS also ran three major seminars at which Paul Dunn talked about the B1G1 Business For Good movement. And not only did Kobomo become a client as a direct result of attending one of those seminars. But the seminar has also profoundly changed the business forever.

Kobomo was a new client of RJS and was seeking to find some sound strategic advice that was not just "rehashed text book stuff". With an awareness of the rapidly changing economic climate, Karen was looking for guidance on how to position Kobomo's unique offering for the long term. And Kylie Anderson was the person she turned to. Through the seminars they hosted with B1G1, Karen had an 'A-ha' moment that resulted in her placing social responsibility as the core value that focuses all her business activities, including her ongoing choice of an accounting firm that has a similar focus on philanthropy at its heart.

B1G1 Business For Good (www.b1g1.com) allows any business, anywhere in the world, to connect with and support good causes anywhere in the world automatically. It does this by carefully selecting and vetting worthy causes, and providing an online platform that makes it remarkably simple and joyful to support them. Importantly, it never focuses on the monetary value of that support. Instead it measures and focuses on its impact i.e. the number of lives that have been made better, one 'micro impact' at a time.

As a result of RJS's introduction to B1G1 Business For Good, Kobomo:

- Has given to worthy causes 864 times: once a day for more than two years, based on the number of items sold that day (the reverse side of every price tag on every item in the shop explains the giving impact that will happen automatically when the item is bought).

- That giving is now done every evening by Karen's 9 year old son using the family computer at home – so he is fully connected with the idea of caring and giving.

- 91,819 people's lives have been made a little bit better by being 'micro-impacted'.

- Those micro impacts include providing 50,478 nourishing meals and 5,733 days of education for disadvantaged children, along with 2,372 days of medical support and 365 days of transport to get them to school.

Karen says, "The people who work with Kobomo are all quite remarkable women who share a desire to have a positive impact in our world. We are friends before colleagues, and our 'work' provides a vehicle of support for each other as well as for others. Yes, we need to sell enough frocks to justify our existence, but it is not the reason we open our doors each day."

However, because they are all passionate about having a positive impact on the world, the Kobomo team is also really keen to sell more frocks (and everything else!). Why? "Because they know that for every extra item they sell, they will help make things better for one more person in need somewhere else in the world."

Kobomo's approach to giving is not 'in your face'. There are no posters or signs around the shop that effectively say, "look at us, aren't we great for doing this". Instead there is a small message on the back of every price tag, and a Free to Shine (see below) donation box next to every till. And their website contains the following message tucked away on the "About us" page:

"Kobomo operates as a 'Business for Good' through our partnership with the remarkable Buy1GIVE1 organisation. That is, for every item we sell we give a meal to a displaced child, or provide extra tuition classes to a girl at risk of being trafficked. This transaction happens daily and you can see the real-time impact we are having on the lives of people who have far less than us."

This message links to their page on www.B1G1.com which quantifies the number of micro impacts they have made (i.e. the same page the numbers quoted above were taken from). NB: Every Business For Good automatically gets their own page quantifying their equivalent numbers.

How it made them feel

"The RJS connection to B1G1, and Kylie's awareness of how it would properly focus my business, resulted in Kobomo's re-birth as a values-centred enterprise. Being a B1G1 Business For Good has given me a profound sense of purpose. It's what I was always looking for, because I always knew that I was supposed to do something more," explains Karen. "It brings such joy to me, my team, my family and my nine-year-old son to know that we really are making a difference. So it's one of many things that I can't thank RJS enough for. They really have changed my life."

Kylie and her team at RJS share the same philosophy. As a result:

- They are also actively involved in the B1G1 Business For Good movement

- Every invoice is sent out with a little business card sized note explaining the giving they will make on behalf of that client, but at the firm's expense, to thank them for being clients

- Each month they honour the promises on those notes by using www. B1G1.com to give a percentage of their turnover

- As a result they have made life a little bit better for 1,504,491 people in need

- Kylie has also co-founded her own charity, Free To Shine, which has already provided education scholarships to prevent 550 young girls in Cambodia becoming victims of sex trafficking (www.freetoshine.org)

- And Free to Shine is now one of the 400+ projects that businesses around the world can support via the B1G1 giving platform

"It's impossible to put a monetary value on the impact of all this on our practice," says Kylie. "But what I do know is that my team are extremely loyal to the firm, extremely proud of what we are doing, and love the fact that they are the ones who decide which causes we give to each month.

"I also know that we continued to grow strongly during the recession, while many of our competitors were really struggling. I'm sure that was because of the loyalty and hard work of my team, and the loyalty of our clients. And I'm sure that our culture of caring and giving was one of the keys to all of that.

"For my part, I am humbled and honoured to be able to make a difference in this way. It's a wonderful feeling."

Generating more profits means this business can support more vulnerable people

Russell Payne & Co. is based in Lincoln, England, and is a one director firm with a team of seventeen. In the last three years it has helped a client to:

- Grow a home-based care franchise from zero to turnover of £1.8 million
- Employ 101 people in a sector facing many cutbacks
- Support hundreds of families struggling to care for vulnerable relatives
- Overcome cashflow challenges that threatened the existence of the business

The client says, "Only as a successful business ourselves can we support the families who need us. Russell and his team have made that happen."

Background information

J&Y Webber Services Ltd. was formed in 2011 by John and Yvonne Webber to purchase and operate a Bluebird Care franchise in central Lincolnshire. Bluebird Care offers home-based care for the elderly, vulnerable and disabled. The business began trading in February 2012.

The situation at the start

John and Yvonne were experienced business people, but were new to the care sector. They had funded the purchase of the franchise with an Enterprise Finance Guarantee loan (EFG) and an overdraft from their bank, and their plan was to grow from zero to sales of £1 million in two years. However, they needed further funds to really take advantage of the potential for growth.

Russell Payne started working with John and Yvonne and within a few months it became clear that a large proportion of their referrals were coming from outside their franchise territory. Rather than turn business away, they needed to purchase a second franchise for the north of the county.

The bank wasn't willing to lend any further funds to a new business without a proven track record. And cashflow was now becoming a problem. Without another source of funding the business was at risk of closing down altogether.

How their accountants helped

Russell introduced John and Yvonne to Victor Finance, a firm of extremely proactive finance brokers. And he worked with them to arrange a small interest-only loan to bridge the pressing cashflow issues, followed by a series of term loans to allow infrastructure improvements and development of the two franchise business units. "Because of our connections, we were able to get a decision and funds for the Webbers within hours," Russell explains "With a loan of £30,000 plus working capital from the existing business the second franchise was quickly up and running."

He continues, "The business was growing quickly, and at the initial business development session with John and Yvonne we identified the need for us to take on the payroll and bookkeeping functions to relieve the pressure on them. They also needed support and guidance to move forward in the right direction. We therefore also agreed to hold quarterly consultancy sessions, together with supporting management information.

"By acting as a virtual FD and conduit for the vast majority of their administrative functions, we relieved much of the time-consuming administrative burden. John and Yvonne could therefore focus on strategy and on marketing the business effectively, ensuring that their operation met the stringent requirements of this highly regulated sector."

However, substantial problems were beginning to emerge, particularly with cashflow. As the business grew, more carers were needed to help service the demand. But the carers were paid on a weekly basis, and cashflow became a major issue as a result of inefficient cash management.

Once again, Russell was able to work with Victor Finance to plug the cash flow gap on a regular basis, often at very short notice.

Turnover had increased, but it soon became clear that profitability was an issue and that the business was producing vanity turnover without an underlying operating profit. "We worked many long hours with the directors to look at pricing," Russell says. "Ultimately we decided that prices had to be set at a premium, considerably above other competitors in the local market, as the quality they were providing was way above the norm."

John and Yvonne found this a very difficult decision to make, but they took Russell's advice and raised their prices by 15%. Only two customers left as a result and profitability increased dramatically.

Russell then recommended that asking customers to pay by direct debit (i.e. where the customer gives the service provider permission to automatically take the amount due directly from their bank account) was the best way to speed up and regularise cashflow.

"Again, this was a difficult process, bearing in mind that the typical customer was receiving domiciliary care and by definition was unlikely to be a long-term customer of the business," Russell says. "However, it was ultimately another key ingredient in ensuring the sustainability of the company as a whole. Alongside the direct debit system the business started to use a virtual credit card terminal, and jointly the two initiatives improved cashflow and reduced their outstanding debtors (i.e. receivables) by 50%."

The difference it made

- Three years on, the growth rate has not slowed and the business now has a turnover of £1.8 million, comfortably exceeding their ambitious initial forecasts.

- John and Yvonne are now looking for a third franchise.

- The business has gone from being a start-up to employing a team of 101.

- They now provide 10,000 hours of much-needed high quality care to 220 clients each year.

With the National Health Service and social services under severe pressure in the UK, John and Yvonne are providing a real alternative to residential care, helping to keep vulnerable people out of hospital and offering a choice to families in the struggle to look after an ageing population.

As Russell says, "Of course, our fees have increased as our client has grown and we currently earn fees of £23,000 a year from them. They also regularly refer people to us and are very much advocates of the practice. But what's really important is that many families across the county now have the reassurance that their family members are receiving a reliable, high quality standard of care, something which is difficult to put a price on."

How it made them feel

John and Yvonne put it this way, "We have been delighted to achieve so much in such a short space of time, and we now feel more confident in the ongoing success of our business. We know we are building on solid foundations, are really excited about expanding our franchise across the county over the coming years, and are forecasting £2 million of sales in the next 12 months.

"None of that would have been possible without our accountant. They prevented cashflow issues causing us to fail before we had hardly even started. They prevented pricing issues from damaging us further down the line. They allowed us to focus on the key strategic issues by taking care of the administrative burden for us. And they allowed us to help hundreds of people in need, and create over 100 brand-new jobs. So in a very real sense, they have changed our lives for the better, and the lives of hundreds of other people too."

The difficult decision that saved this business from going under

Taggart & Partners is a single director firm with a team of eight, based in Brisbane, Australia, that has helped a client:

- Save a profitable business from going under when a new venture failed
- Cut their tax bill by 55%, from $250,000 to $114,000
- Repay $500,000 owed to creditors
- Buy a house for the first time

"I cannot imagine running a business without their support," says the client. "They go way above and beyond a regular accountancy firm."

Background information

The client is a unique, award-winning cocktail bar in Brisbane, Australia. Founded in 2003, it was the first of its kind in the city and has proved to be an extremely popular concept. The business currently employs seven people and turns over in the region of $1.5 million.

The situation at the start

In 2008, after trading successfully for five years, the business owners decided to diversify and open a luxury restaurant and nightclub together with a local celebrity chef. The chef had no funding to open his own restaurant but there were very few establishments of this kind in the city so it seemed an ideal opportunity to fill a gap in the market.

However, the business owners...

- Did very little research into the viability of the new business

- Had little or no experience in the restaurant industry

- Didn't seek out any business advice before launching and had no cashflow forecasts and no fit-out budget

The chef himself had no business experience but nonetheless, the two business partners each contributed $500,000 to set up the new venture.

By 2010, the restaurant was employing a team of 35 with a turnover in the region of $1.1 million, and a trading loss of $517,000.

The time and energy the business owners put into the new business meant that they had lost focus on their core business, the cocktail bar, and it had started to experience difficulties.

Most of the initial $1 million investment had gone and the owners were relying on loans from family to fund the business. They also owed $250,000 in tax.

Not surprisingly, they were finding the situation extremely stressful with no idea what to do for the best.

How their accountants helped

This was how Raymond Taggart found things when he first became their business advisor.

"Neither of the two partners had fully appreciated the potential impact that the launch of the restaurant business would have on so many fronts," he comments. "Once they realized that not only was the new venture in trouble, but that all their hard work building the core business into a thriving success was also in jeopardy, the stress they found themselves under was unimaginable."

Raymond started by helping them to regain focus and control of the core business and also made systematic efforts to mitigate the losses incurred by the restaurant operation.

As well as the unpaid tax bill, trade creditors exceeded $500,000 so the most pressing issue was to organise a payment plan. "We negotiated payment arrangements with their outstanding creditors and also negotiated a highly favourable agreement with the Australian Taxation Office to reduce the debt by 55% to just $114,000," Raymond explains.

"We then worked with the client to establish a 3-way business plan and a cash flow forecast and helped them to restructure the management team. We undertook a full review of the business model including the menu offering, the number of nightly covers, opening hours etc. with the aim of migrating away from the highly unprofitable, expensive degustation menu and trying to return the restaurant business to profitability."

Unfortunately, what became apparent to Raymond as a result of the review was that the restaurant simply wasn't viable. The kind of clientele they needed just didn't fit the demographics of the location.

"It's always an incredibly difficult conversation to have with people who have made a significant financial and emotional investment in a business venture. It's very hard for them to accept that they may have made a mistake," Raymond says.

"Part of our role was to show the client the impact of not cutting their losses and what the worst case scenario looked like. We were able to draw on our experiences of working with other restaurants to highlight the risks involved.

"In the end, the scenario planning made the decision something of a 'no-brainer' when it became obvious that prolonging the new business venture would ultimately mean sacrificing the hard work that had gone into building up the cocktail bar.

"Ultimately the client saw our role as not simply that of their accountant, but also as a trusted business advisor who had their best interests at heart. We reassured them every step of the way that if they followed our advice, we could rescue the core business from bankruptcy."

While this was not the outcome they had hoped for when they embarked on their new venture, the business owners recognized that closing it down was the best option.

The difference it made

Once the decision was made to close the restaurant and nightclub, Raymond and the business owners were able to focus on the profitability of the cocktail bar. As a result it now runs far more efficiently and has the same level of turnover with a team of seven as when it employed 18.

How it made them feel

Raymond adds, "It was a huge relief for the business owners to be able to pay off creditors and repay the loans from family members. We're also in the process of working with one of the partners, who has led the recovery of the business, to facilitate and negotiate the exit of the other business owner. And for her, the peace of mind knowing that the cocktail bar is on a solid foundation matters just as much as the financial side."

And the final piece of good news is that the remaining business owner has been able to buy her own house – something that would have been unthinkable just a few years ago.

This client's message for business owners is 'Spend more on your accountant – it's worth it'

Tayabali Tomlin, a three-director firm with a team of eighteen based in Cheltenham, England that has helped a client:

- Recover from the sudden disappearance of £500,000 from the bank balance
- Identify and start to recoup £750,000 of uncollected membership fees
- Win the support of its customers and keep trading throughout the financial difficulties
- Save the reputation of the high profile business owner

"I wish dearly that my previous accountant had given me the same level of support I've had from the Tayabali Tomlin team," the client says now.

Background information

The Entrepreneurs Circle was founded by Nigel Botterill in 2010 and provides training, guidance, help and support to small businesses that want to grow. As a membership organisation, it specialises in helping its members find and keep customers and is at the cutting edge of modern marketing. Turnover is approximately £5m and the business employs 60 people.

The situation at the start

In 2011 Nigel had taken on a qualified accountant as a full time employee, hoping to gain many advantages from having this kind of expertise permanently available. As a result, he had also downgraded the service he bought from his external accountants so that in effect, they just rubber stamped the reports produced by in-house team. "But by late 2014," says Nigel, "I was becoming concerned that I wasn't getting all the support and information I needed. While much of this was due to the rapid growth of the business and the fact that the finance team was severely stretched, I felt I needed more input."

Seeking more added value services, he approached Tayabali Tomlin to help the business.

CEO Aynsley Damery describes what made Nigel choose them. "We have a unique approach for entrepreneurs and look to change their lives by helping them grow and scale sustainably, improve profits, reduce tax bills and plan for exit. We only work with clients for whom we can create significant value. To determine whether we're the right accountants for our prospective clients, we interview them in advance so we can get a feel for each other, making it quite clear that if someone is looking for compliance only they are unlikely to be the right client for us.

"We obtain a copy of the company's last set of financial statements and latest management accounts and budgets, if available. We then benchmark them against competitors and those in a similar field, run their numbers through our profit improvement software, look at the tax structure and potential quick wins and create a key possibilities report."

Initially Aynsley and his team were tasked to review the financial systems. The review highlighted numerous areas where systems needed significant improvement, but Nigel was confident that with his level of oversight, sign off and overall control review there was no risk to the business.

"We covered the lack of management accounts at this point," Aynsley says. "In retrospect Nigel admits that although he had asked the right questions and had ostensibly been given the right answers, he should have looked for more evidence to support the explanations he had been given rather than just accepting them at face value."

With the level of insight the review had provided for Aynsley, he felt that everything was under control. But all that changed with one phone call from Nigel.

"He had logged on to his internet banking system to authorise a few payments and was horrified to find that the bank account was more than £500,000 short of where he thought it would be," Aynsley remembers. "Instead of the balance of almost £700,000 he was expecting there was only £150,000 in the account and he was due to pay a £250,000 VAT bill within the next two days."

Nigel adds, "I would consider myself to be financially astute. I thought I knew what it takes to run a successful business. To find ourselves in this position was simply devastating."

How their accountants helped

Aynsley was actually in India (on a B1G1 study tour) when he took Nigel's call, but his team immediately leapt into action.

While the initial thought was that the money had been stolen, their forensic investigation uncovered very poor levels of financial control and the ultimate root cause – uncollected income of almost £750,000.

"Large inflows of cash from the advance sale of convention tickets and training academy annual passes had masked a significant issue with the regular collection of core membership subscriptions," Aynsley explains. "As the business grew rapidly in 2014 and the number of employees doubled, the focus had been on expanding the top line. But operational rigour fell well short of where it needed to be and it was now clear that a business of this size lacked the controls to ensure that the growth was safe, secure and sustainable."

The team helped with the urgent cashflow problems and were able to negotiate time to pay the VAT bill with HMRC. Then they developed a workable reporting structure with a list of daily, weekly and monthly reports and a list of tasks for the members of the finance team.

"We looked at the division of responsibilities," Aynsley continues, "and putting into place the numerous recommendations from our initial management report. We instigated a series of cost cutting measures and looked carefully at their impact on the business model. Further cashflow measures were introduced and Nigel injected more of his own money, with a small level of further borrowing."

However, as more and more past invoices emerged and income didn't rise to the required level, it became clear that they needed to take more drastic action. As Aynsley comments, "Failing to collect £750,000 would be a hard problem to overcome for any company."

A Company Voluntary Arrangement (CVA) seemed to offer a solution. With creditors paid back over a fixed period, it allows a business to continue to trade – something that was crucial to Nigel and his reputation.

"We introduced Nigel to an insolvency practitioner, who is also a long standing client of ours. Together we looked at all the various options and worked and re-worked the numbers. We looked at the pros and cons of the options and provided guidance, acting as a sounding board for Nigel and his senior team. They were keen to ensure that every creditor was paid in full and that no one would lose any money."

The difference it made

- Daily cash reporting, weekly debtors and creditor reports are now happening as a matter of routine.

- Management accounts and board packs are being prepared on a monthly basis. Reporting of actual versus budget and analysis of variances, significant items of expenditure and commentary on unusual items is discussed between the management team and with Tayabali Tomlin.

- Balance sheet movements, working capital management and key ratios are being monitored and graphed. Key performance indicators, identified during the business and financial model work, are being measured, reported on and shared with the team.

- Controls and key system improvements highlighted in the management report are being actioned.

- Profit is increasing significantly and with the final cost cutting phase implemented and revenue on a strong growth curve, the future profitability and cash position of the company looks far more secure.

- The team feels rejuvenated and has developed plans for further profitable income streams: a new improved training academy and sales of online training and vault contents to overseas markets.

- The potential for exiting the CVA earlier than expected is now a possibility. "However, as it will be difficult to obtain funding with the current credit scoring issues, it may be more prudent to keep to the agreed proposals and use any excess cash to scale sustainably and profitably," Aynsley comments, adding, "We have ultimately saved the company from going bust and directly saved a large number of jobs. Indirectly we have saved even more."

How it made them feel

Now that the nightmare is coming to an end, Nigel has a simple message for business owners: "Spend more on your accountant. It's worth it because low levels of fees mean low levels of support and a lack of attention to the business.

"At the beginning it was like a physical blow had been struck to my solar plexus and it had a hugely negative effect that seeped into every waking hour. Having to put on a brave face, managing it and the implications of it sucked hours out of every day.

"What made the difference for me was the phone calls I had with Aynsley. He showed me that if I handled the situation well it could actually enhance our standing with our customers and it wouldn't diminish the business. He persuaded me to make a video explaining what had happened and to release that to our customers. Within 48 hours of the video going live I'd had 271 letters and messages, all of them very supportive and many of them telling me that they had dealt with similar problems themselves.

"What has come out of this isn't just the continuation of the Entrepreneurs Circle. This kind of cashflow issue affects many businesses but it isn't talked about. Business owners are typically ashamed to admit to it. By bringing it into the open – and we now run workshops and webinars on the subject and have produced a guide for our members – hundreds of small businesses have started to tackle the problem, saving more jobs and creating more wealth."

Spending three times as much with accountants who changed their lives

A three director firm with a team of eleven based in Leeds, England that has helped a client:

- Protect two directors from personal bankruptcy and the loss of their homes
- Save businesses in three cities from closure and retain more than 80 jobs
- Increase profits by 237%
- Obtain finance for a £1.5 million management buy-out and for future expansion

The client says, "We spend 3 times what we used to with our accountants and it's worth every penny."

Background information

MOJO started in 1996 in Leeds and the business now has two other sites in Manchester and Liverpool. With the slogan of 'Music for the people; food for the soul; good times forever' they have built a core following for their bars in all three cities. Originally the business had three owners who were each responsible for their own areas, but it is now run by just two, Martin and Mal.

The situation at the start

In 2011 a shareholder dispute arose which resulted in one of the owners leaving the business. However, what began as a relatively straightforward matter became increasingly acrimonious as the departing shareholder demanded to be bought out. Mediation did not work out and Martin and Mal were left to find £1.5 million to complete the buyout. Worse still, if they couldn't raise the finance they would face personal bankruptcy and the loss of their homes as well as closure of the business.

"The stress of the situation meant that I was constantly anxious and depressed," Martin recalls. "I even lost two stone in weight. And despite being told that this type of case never went to court, that's exactly what happened. The only person saying you can get through this was Jonathan Myers."

How their accountants helped

Urquhart Warner Myers ('UWM') partner Jonathan had been the accountant for MOJO since 2008 and had already helped them to navigate their way through a difficult PAYE compliance check. "We also moved from just doing annual accounts to monthly management accounts to get a true feel of what was happening in the business throughout the trading year rather than after the year end had passed. We introduced Xero cloud accounting and a One Page Plan for the business so they had a lot of up-to-date information available," he says.

Coincidentally a week before the court hearing in autumn 2013, UWM were running a special seminar for their clients and prospects, called 'How to get an extra £2.2 million in your business and personal bank accounts.' Although he was snowed under with preparation for the court case and was ready to cancel his place, Martin made the effort to attend. And it turned out to be a pivotal moment for the whole business.

In fact, Martin sent Jonathan this email straight after the seminar.

> *Hi Jonathan*
>
> *Just wanted to drop you a quick email to say thank you for today's seminar. It was truly inspirational. As you well know things have been pretty rough now for a while and today managed to refocus me on what is required going forward.*
> *Please sign us up for the plan and do it quickly!!*
>
> *Martin*

Together with Mal they started using UWM's Performance Measurement and Improvement ('PMI') system to work on the future of the business. Jonathan explains what they did:

"Soon after the £2m seminar and the court hearing, we ran a GoalGetter Day with both directors of the company (*GoalGetter is a software tool that helps to identify and set goals for business owners*). At the end of this session both the directors and UWM had clarity over the company's vision and goals together with the directors' own personal goals. This process led very easily into the next stage of building a One Page Plan for each bar.

"With goals set and the One Page Plan complete, in January 2014 we started monthly BoardView meetings with the whole management team. Sitting in on board meetings and acting as the trusted outsider brought a level of engagement that hadn't existed previously. We now review the One Page Plan with the whole team and plan ahead for the business much further into the future than before."

As the court case and the process of buying-out the previous partner continued, Jonathan began to implement other changes.

"In 2014, we rolled out Receipt Bank to handle purchase invoices and expense claims and also introduced Crunchboards. This allowed the business to get very detailed reporting on KPIs bar by bar. For example, we set up boards to report on certain cost centres as a % of turnover, separated by bar. This enabled us to look at areas where there were variations across the bars and because the data is updated three times a day, there is no involvement needed from the company. They just log in and see the latest data."

Jonathan also found a corporate finance firm to handle the financing of the court settlement. "The firm carrying out the financing due diligence spent time both with ourselves and the directors. They were impressed with the amount of information available readily from Xero, the (mainly non-financial) KPIs on the One Page Plan at a company level and at a bar level together with internal bar by bar information on the company's intranet. This information really helped with the due diligence process."

The difference it made

The PMI planning process that Martin and Mal had signed up to as a result of the seminar meant looking at many KPIs that had not previously been measured.

For example:

- Team happiness – this led to managers at two bars leaving and increased morale among the remaining teams.
- Guest happiness – highlighted areas that guests were happy with and areas that the company could devote more attention to. In particular, the pricing questions showed which bars had guests that were very price sensitive and which were less sensitive. The consequence of this was that in the price sensitive bars the pricing was untouched and elsewhere prices were increased. Special offers were discontinued in all bars.

- They also set targets for and increased GP%, double sales and reduced stock wastage.

- They set targets and monitored spend per transaction, number of transactions, number of new guests, standards and training audits, social media activity and mystery visits.

Finally, in the summer of 2014, the court case was concluded and the buyout of the previous partner was finalised. Martin comments, "The systems and level of reporting that Jonathan had helped to put in place played a large part in obtaining the finance we needed."

In addition to this:

- Profits for 2014 increased by 237% over 2013. 2015 profits are projected to increase again by 40% over the 2014 results.

- Gross profit increased by 25.5%.

- The management is now more structured with defined roles for everyone.

- Both directors now have the time they want to spend with their families and on their leisure pursuits.

- They no longer face the threat of losing their homes.

- The company's expansion plans that were put on hold during the dispute are now moving ahead and financing for new bars is already in place.

How it made them feel

With a complex and acrimonious dispute to contend with, morale at MOJO was very low. But working with Jonathan on the PMI plan changed everything for Martin and Mal. As Jonathan says:

"As soon as the PMI process started, they felt they had clarity about:

- What the business was doing at the start point
- What the business needed to do to achieve the vision and goals established at the GoalGetter day
- What steps they could take to achieve these goals

"They now understand:

- That the increased turnover, gross profit and net profit comes as a result of the changes (some small, some large) that we have implemented and continue to fine tune on a regular basis

- That guests come to them for a great fun night out, not to buy the cheapest drinks in town. Making it fun is the key to more people visiting the bars and staying for longer

- That they are more in tune with what their guests want

- That they have a more engaged team"

The owners have a huge sense of relief that the uncertainty and stress of the past is over and that the future of the business is secure.

Martin puts it this way, "This was my first experience of working with an accountant who looks to the future, not the past. And by saving our business and our homes, they have literally changed our lives. As a result we now spend three times what we used to with our accountants and it's worth every penny!"

Unravelling a financial nightmare secured the future for an Alzheimer's sufferer and his wife

A sole practitioner based in the Wirral, UK who has helped a client:

- Untangle a difficult and distressing situation
- Gain a full insurance settlement that means peace of mind for the future
- Reach an 'unbelievable' arrangement with HMRC
- Have the financial security to give up work to care for her ill husband

Alan Woods comments, "I'm so proud that we were able to help this client who was struggling with a fiscal nightmare and didn't know where to turn for help."

Background information

Gary Williams was an IT support professional offering IT consultancy for businesses. The business had been trading for a number of years and turned over around £150,000. Gary lives in Halifax with his wife Jean Westacott.

The situation at the start

Gary had been diagnosed with Alzheimer's and was unable to continue working. He had previously taken out an insurance policy that covered his illness, but he didn't have the accounts required by the insurers to satisfy their payment criteria. One of the symptoms of his condition was his inability to deal with financial matters and this had resulted in a fiscal nightmare that was complicated and difficult to resolve.

Jean was trying to produce the relevant information for the insurers but was finding it hard, particularly as Gary couldn't remember the name of his accountant.

Although her husband had done the right thing by taking out the insurance policy, Jean was increasingly frustrated that, because his earnings were lower when he made a claim than when he took out the policy, the amount of benefit was being unfairly restricted.

How their accountants helped

Jean had posted on a website called Choose Your Accountant, explaining her situation and asking if anyone could help.

Alan and his team saw the post and immediately wanted to get involved. Alan explained to Jean that he was willing to help at no charge to see what had or hadn't been done. "We didn't start this process with any intention of making money from the client; we just wanted to see if we could help them get what they were owed from their insurance company."

From the accounts, bank statements and sales invoices that Jean supplied Alan estimated that Gary's business activity in his earlier years (as a sole trader) was significantly higher than when his health had started to deteriorate. The limited company accounts that Jean had submitted to their insurance company were from the later (lower earning) period, so this finding could have a significant impact on the pay-out.

Alan offered to recreate the accounts for the 3 years Gary was a sole trader, liaise with the insurance company on their behalf and to deal with any matters arising with HMRC too.

"We spoke to Angela at Scottish Provident (the insurance company) to confirm that, if we were able to provide accounts that showed an improved position for the earlier years, this would result in a larger pay-out by the insurer. Angela confirmed this was the case in her letter to Jean dated 26 April 2013. Jean was delighted to get this confirmation from the insurers, as were we.

"After receiving this confirmation we set about preparing the accounts from the limited information provided to us. We had spoken to HMRC and they had no record of any information for Gary as a sole trader so these accounts had obviously never been prepared before."

Once the accounts were agreed by Jean and Gary, Alan sent them to Scottish Provident. They confirmed that Gary would receive a higher percentage of his full insured benefit and his payments were increased by £300 per month.

This was good news of course, but Alan wasn't satisfied that this was the maximum amount Gary was due. He asked Scottish Provident if there was anything else that would influence the pay-out. They explained that in some situations they are able to go back further to see what the true income levels were for the business before the illness took full effect.

This was exactly what Alan needed. "We liaised again with Jean to see if there was any more information she could give us. She was able to supply a further 3 years' worth of records and we prepared the sole trader accounts and tax returns. We submitted this updated information to Angela at Scottish Provident and then we got the best news ever!"

The initial result had been reviewed and the amount of the pay-out was increased by over £1,300 per month. It was also backdated to when Gary had first started to claim, giving him and Jean an additional £30,000. And they were also due a £250,000 lump sum.

Needless to say, Jean was very, very happy!

There was one piece of rather less good news. Alan had submitted the missing tax returns to HMRC (the UK tax authority) and this triggered a tax liability of £25,000. While this didn't diminish the results Alan had achieved, it did create another issue to be resolved.

Alan was able to negotiate a payment plan with HMRC. "We prepared a household forecast and explained the situation with Gary's health. HMRC agreed that Jean could pay off the liability at £200 per month."

In summary, the work that Alan and his team did for Jean and Gary was:

- Initial review of position
- Contacted previous accountants to gather details available
- Contacted HMRC to confirm what information had been submitted
- Prepared four years of sole trader accounts (two years of limited company accounts had already been prepared and provided by Jean)
- Prepared and submitted six Self Assessment Tax Returns
- Agreed payment plan with HMRC
- Dealt with all ongoing correspondence from HMRC
- Liaised with Scottish Provident
- Provided support and reassurance to Jean so that she could concentrate on looking after Gary without the worry of dealing with the finances as well

- Countless letters, e-mails and phone calls to HMRC, Scottish Provident and Jean

The difference it made

The situation for the client at the end of the process was hugely improved:

- Increase of £1,300 in monthly income (£2,000 to £3,300) via the insurance policy

- Backdated adjustment of approx. £25k when the additional information was provided

- Jean was able to give up work to enable her to care for her husband full-time

- She went back to university to take a Masters in Counselling

Although fees were not a primary factor in helping Jean and Gary, the firm did earn £5,000 + VAT from the work. But as Alan says, "It was much more important for us to make a difference in this case than it was to make a profit."

How it made them feel

When Alan first made contact with Jean she was trying to care for her husband and tackle the complexities of his financial affairs. Understandably, she was becoming stressed and increasingly desperate to find a solution. Once the insurance settlement was in place, she wrote this testimonial for Alan.

"Alan Woods is the perfect combination of the consummate professional combined with a human side that is both compassionate and practical. He was patient and very supportive whilst the process was progressing and liaised regularly with myself and the external agencies. Alan was extremely tenacious on our behalf and we finally received a full settlement from the insurance company which has enabled us to enjoy a level of financial security which without Alan's unwavering support we would have been unable to secure.

"Alan even arranged for a box of my favourite wine to be delivered so that we could celebrate when the nightmare had finally receded. Without Alan's kindness, efficiency and empathetic consideration I would have struggled both emotionally and financially during this very challenging time. "

"The client didn't even know if she was making a profit"

A one partner firm with a team of seven based in Hampshire, England that has helped a client:

- Fulfil her ambitions by opening new premises with projected turnover of £2 million a year
- Add £50,000 to her bank account
- Resolve a long running dispute with her neighbour
- Simplify accounting systems so her customers have complete transparency about their payments
- Halve the number of debtors

Guy Robinson, Xebra MD, says: "Her creativity and passion has no limits, and we believe we have given her the financial capability and insight to achieve her amazing visions for the future."

Background information

Hartley House is based in Winchester and comprises a day nursery (Casa) and a nursery school (Lido). There is also a nursery and infant school at Norman Court, near Salisbury as well as a new outdoor activity centre with boarding for more than 100 children. Within the Casa building there is also a Montessori Training Centre.

The combined businesses trade as a limited company, with a turnover of around £600,000 per year, and a small profit after the director's remuneration.

The situation at the start

Susan, the business owner, wasn't happy with the support and help she was getting from their previous bookkeeper/accountant. She did not understand her accounts, or the reason why they were making the low returns achieved over the years. As a result, in 2010 the business moved to Xebra Accounting.

When Guy Robinson, MD at Xebra, first met Susan he realised that although she was clearly not motivated by money, she was frustrated that she could not achieve her own visions, because the results from the business did not enable any expansion to take place. She also had a third nursery at the time, and did not know whether it was making any money.

To make matters worse, a dispute with her neighbours was also causing problems, as it involved a very high wall, and the neighbour was the Church of England!

Responsibility for the finances, invoicing and many other administration tasks lay with Susan's right-hand team member, Lorraine. At the initial meeting it was apparent to Guy that Lorraine had a very complicated way of doing things that no-one other than Lorraine understood.

Guy quickly discovered that:

- the business effectively had six departments, but no financial information as to the profitability of any department

- there was no plan for the current financial year

- the finances were supported by a plethora of loans, all with different terms and rates

- there was an urgent need for some investment in IT

- amounts due from customers were much too high, and there was a large pile of 'disputed' fees

- Susan had been forced to inject the business with her own money twice recently so that the wages bill could be met

How their accountants helped

With accounts previously being prepared 6 months or more after the year end, Guy immediately tried to establish a timetable for Lorraine to produce basic management information on a monthly basis. This meant buying a couple of new computers, which he helped to find finance for, as the bank was unwilling to lend more.

Lorraine soon complained that she did not have time to do the management accounts because she was dealing with parent queries 'all the time'.

"We looked into this further," Guy says, "and found that she billed at the end of the month for every session booked for that child that month, using a complex series of spreadsheets. However, parents were given information about their bookings weekly, so they never tied into the monthly invoices. Customers paying a monthly amount, which was an estimate of their annual bill divided by 12, further complicated the situation. As no statements were issued, one can imagine the chaos caused for parents!

"To further complicate things, additions such as lunches for whole day attendance were billed separately, with parents being credited for any that weren't taken for whatever reason.

"Unsurprisingly, there were dozens of queries every month, and cash flow was poor as the business was billing so far in arrears."

Guy recommended that they changed to billing in advance for booked sessions, that lunches and other extras were built into the fees, that absences be payable unless otherwise agreed, and that extra sessions were billed separately as taken. From over 100 parents, only two complained about the consolidation of the lunch cost – more actually said it made the fees easier to understand.

"We also recommended sales ledger accounts for every child, so that monthly payments could be allocated and a statement issued and also suggested that, as the next stage of the changes, Susan move all her clients to online direct debit collections."

Over the next six months, Lorraine struggled to work with the new systems, but with plenty of support from Guy and his team, she began to make headway. However, there was a need to get financial information more quickly than she could produce. Guy started a project to speed things up by moving all the accounting over to Xero, but that was the final straw for Lorraine and she left.

"We took up the baton," Guy says. "We persuaded Susan that once converted to Xero the bookkeeping time would diminish significantly, and we could distribute most of it amongst the existing team and ourselves. Susan now has management accounts available whenever she needs them, as the accounts are effectively 'real time'. We prepare financial reports from Xero on a monthly basis."

The difference it made

Susan now has time to lead the business more effectively and work on developing her vision for the future:

- She has launched a new nursery in the grounds of a former private school (Norman Court) near Salisbury.

- She has also opened an outdoor adventure and activity centre, with a £2 million contract over the next 3 years with the Department of Education, to provide outdoor and country experiences to city children, as part of the national curriculum.

- In September 2016 she will re-open the former Norman Court secondary school.

- As a result of the financial information Xebra was able to produce, she has closed the small nursery which was proven to be making losses.

In addition:

- Turnover of the combined operations is expected to grow rapidly over the next 3 years, probably in excess of £2 million.

- Client contact has improved and parents are happier with the more transparent link between their payments and the sessions actually taken.

- Debtors have been halved.

- There is about £50,000 more in the bank, enabling Casa to be redecorated and a new baby room converted in the attic.

- The teaching staff at all locations now have more information available to them to help them do their jobs and the children have benefitted from additional investment in facilities and teaching materials through the financing obtained.

- Xebra took on the payroll, a challenging job as there are around 150 people on the payroll, but only a fraction of them work in any given week.

- Xebra helped Susan tackle the pension auto enrolment process, another challenging job.

- And Guy even helped to resolve the problem with the high wall and the Church of England! "We eventually helped to find an amicable solution with the land owner. We were involved in liaising with other professionals, and raising finances to cover the remedial work."

The fees Xebra earns have also increased from £2,365 in 2010 to more than £20,000 in 2015. But, as Guy says, "More importantly than that, we have had some fabulous opportunities to work with Susan in developing systems, teaching her team how to use them, and seeing them actually working. Many members of our team have done tasks they have never done before and by getting really involved, they now understand the business from the inside."

How it made them feel

The difference for Susan has been astonishing. "Without Guy's support, help and inspiration I simply couldn't have achieved what I have. I thought that the dreams I had for my business might never become a reality, but with a huge amount of effort and enthusiasm from Guy and everyone at Xebra they are actually starting to happen."

Brief inspirational stories

Giving £10 million of professional services for free

AfID is an award winning UK-based social enterprise that since 2009 has helped accountants to:

- Give over £10 million worth of professional support
- To over 400 charities and non-profit organisations
- Make a sustainable difference to people in need in 50 countries across the world

"Accountants always get back so much more than they give," says its founder.

AfID (www.afid.org.uk) gives accountants the opportunity to use their financial skills as volunteers on a wide range of assignments lasting from two weeks to permanent placements. For example, budgeting with a street child centre in Kampala, coaching a hospital bookkeeper in Kigali or financial reporting for a primary school in Kathmandu.

Founder Neil Jennings explains, "Our aim is to develop and enhance the skills, confidence and potential of local people, in order to give the charities and non-profits we support the financial management capacity they need to deliver more effective and sustainable programmes."

"Because all of our volunteers are accountants, there is really good continuity from one volunteer to the next. Consequently, real results can be achieved in a far shorter time frame than is possible with other traditional voluntary placements. And this means that even career-minded professionals with full-time jobs can get involved and make a very real difference in as little as a couple of weeks."

The evidence that they really can make a difference is evident in the numbers. AfID volunteers have given:

- 225,000 pro-bono hours
- Equivalent to more than £10 million of professional services

- Supporting over 400 charities and non-profit organisations in 50 countries

Crucially, 99.3% of recipients say that all of that voluntary support has delivered exactly what AfID promised – because their local finance teams are now more confident and better able to perform their duties.

In addition the 900 volunteer accountants who have given so much since 2009 say it has also made a profound difference to them personally:

- 98% now feel more open minded
- 97% feel more resourceful
- 97% feel more comfortable with unfamiliar situations
- 96% feel more culturally sensitive
- 96% feel better able to adapt to varied and challenging work environments
- 93% feel more confident
- 92% feel they have developed skills that are improving their performance at work
- 87% feel better equipped to manage change

Neil adds, "I always tell accountants not to think for one minute that just because they'll be working on serious issues that it won't be fun. Many of our volunteers are surprised at how much they genuinely have in common with those they came to help, and how much laughter they share together. They certainly get inspired by the whole experience. And they always get back so much more than they give."

Creating 20 jobs by staying professional when losing a client

Auroma Accounting is a 10 person company in Mumbai, India that has helped a client to:

- Amicably dissolve a partnership that wasn't working
- Start a new business that works so well that it has already created 20 jobs
- Attract some of the world's biggest companies as clients

"It has been a really rewarding journey for us too, since our fee is now three times what it was when the business started," says the firm's founder.

"Without our help," says Auroma Accounting's founder Niraj Pande, "one of the best known public relations consultancies in India probably wouldn't exist, and neither would the jobs of the 20 people who work there.

"Originally we were appointed by a different two partner PR firm. Their accounts had got in a mess, so we stepped in to provide end-to-end accounting support that sorted it all out. But the partnership had an inherent flaw: the young and free-spirited personalities of the two partners. It was not long before there were clashes of opinion and they decided to go their separate ways.

"We were about to lose an important client, but we still did everything we could to ensure an amicable dissolution settlement between the two partners. And because we remained professional at that point, the story then took a very positive turn for everybody.

"One of the partners decided that they wanted to set up their own PR firm, but was very apprehensive about the financial implications of going solo. So we produced a very detailed set of profit and cash flow projections, which we used to give them the reassurance that they needed. Equally importantly we also reminded them of their skills, strengths, and successes in order to help them believe in themselves. And we promised that we would always be there to help out and advise, and even offered to support them by discounting our fees for the first six months.

"As accountants we obviously help our clients understand the numbers. But we shouldn't underestimate the importance of the role we also play in giving them moral support, reassurance, self-belief and confidence. In this case those things made all the difference. And as a result our client started a business which is now one of the best known public relations firms in India, employing more than 20 staff and handling some of the biggest international brands.

"It has been a really rewarding journey for us too, since our fee is now three times what it was when the business started. We have also derived immense satisfaction from being part of their success story, and the other partner in the original business has now also asked us to be the accountants for their new business too. So doing the right thing, even when you are in the process of losing a client, definitely pays off."

Building deeper and more mutually rewarding relationships

The Wellington, New Zealand office of leading global network BDO has helped clients to:

- Dramatically improve turnover and profits, and
- Meet their ambitious targets
- By focusing on the numbers that really matter

"A KPI monitoring and discussion approach is the key to deeper and more mutually rewarding relationships with clients," says Andrew MacDonell.

Senior manager Andrew MacDonell believes there is no substitute for getting in front of businesses, being persistent and using their KPIs as the basis for more productive, impactful and profitable conversations, and forging deeper relationships.

"Zephyr Consulting first came to us for some company car tax planning advice, but they were outraged when we sent them a $500 bill for it, calculating what it equated to as a cost per word for the advice letter that accompanied it. So it wasn't a promising start! But seven years later we have helped them to grow their turnover from a post GFC related low of $3.5 million to almost $11 million. In fact, the relationship is now so strong that we always go out for dinner with them after our regular meetings, and they have asked us to help them create a personal financial strategy to help their children get on the housing ladder," explains Andrew.

"They also introduced us to Integration Works, who were frustrated with their Big Four accountants who kept giving them a long list of technical options, rather than getting off the fence and recommending a particular course of action. But again, it wasn't a promising start, because they failed to turn up to the first three meetings we organised. So in the end I had to engineer an accidental meeting in the pub one evening. And since then we have helped them to finally start meeting their ambitious monthly profit targets, tap into exciting global opportunities, have a plan for achieving their personal goals and put in place a tax efficient remuneration strategy. "

The keys to their success

In both cases the key things Andrew has done to help create this success have included:

- **Setting them up with cloud accounting** – "so that they always have access to reliable real-time numbers."

- **Creating dashboards** – using a cloud tool (CrunchBoards) that, at the push of a button, presents all the key numbers in a very simple, highly visual and easily understood way. "It is so powerful and easy to use that we are starting to use it with all of our clients. But actually, the exact tool you use to give clients their KPIs isn't the most important thing. If the client is happier with the familiarity of an A3 spreadsheet, as one of ours is, then that's what we will use. Focusing on KPIs matters far more than which piece of technology you use to do it."

- **Meeting at least every two months to discuss the key numbers** – "These meetings are invaluable, so we do whatever it takes to make them happen. With Integration Works, for example, that means we run them as 'CrunchBoards and breakfast' meetings at 7:15 AM on Friday mornings."

Some of the key areas the meetings focus on include:

- Reviewing product, customer and departmental profitability – "for example, by identifying that one department was particularly profitable, we were able to help them achieve a $300,000 turnaround in profitability for the business as a whole, by putting more emphasis on that department."

- Monitoring understanding and trends

- Challenging costs

- Identifying what is and isn't working

- Creating action plans, and

- Ensuring full accountability so that action plans are turned into action and results

"Personally I don't believe you can commoditise this kind of approach, because it should evolve and lead into specialist areas and advice that can't possibly be envisaged or included in a fixed price at the outset. But I do passionately believe that a periodic KPI monitoring and discussion approach is the key to deeper and more mutually rewarding relationships with clients."

Simple things that generated more success than the client dared to imagine

Clarand Accountants is a two director firm in Corbridge, England that has helped a client to:

- Increase sales by 169%
- Double the size of their team
- Finally feel in control

"Their advice has been crucial to our success," says the client.

Annie Barr Associates trains nurses and healthcare professionals. They started trading in 2009, and by 2012, despite working with three different accountants in three years, they still had no proper accounting or filing systems.

"All they wanted when they appointed us was up-to-date and timely information," explains Clarand director Claire Priestley. In response Clarand:

- Set them up with cloud accounting software – which the client understands, and really values as she can access it via her mobile phone

- Gave them, for the first time ever, complete clarity over their outstanding creditors and debtors – which made it easier to keep suppliers happy, collect the money owed by customers and get cashflow fully under control

- Created a simple filing system – so that paperwork could be found quickly and easily

- Obtained grant funding to train and support the office manager – so that, despite not previously knowing what a debit or credit was, she could take responsibility for many aspects of the company's finances

- Calculated the true costs of running the company's various training courses – which allowed them to address profitability issues

- Established that the client is exempt from VAT (the tax on sales) – which greatly simplified the accounting and administrative burden

- Helped them understand how a limited company works, how to take dividends properly and how to use retained profits to their advantage

"To us accountants that probably all seems very simple and basic, but to clients it can make a profound difference. And it certainly did in this case, since in the three years we have worked with them their turnover has increased by 169%, they have more than doubled the size of their team and their cash flow is now firmly under control," says Claire.

"Three years ago they were confident that the business would be a success, but simply couldn't understand how the money side of it worked, and consequently felt stressed, anxious and completely out of control. Recently, however, Annie told me that she feels in control of the business for the first time since its incorporation, and that our support and guidance has given her the confidence to take it forward way beyond her initial expectations."

Annie Barr herself says, "I have never worked with accountants with so much care and attention to every detail of my business. They go beyond what I would have expected from accountants. Their advice has been crucial to our success."

Turning managers into business owners

Clear Vision, a two director practice based in a market town in Wiltshire, England, has helped:

- One client to sell his business
- Realise the dreams of two of his senior managers
- Transform the happiness of everyone involved

"Having a really good accountant has been instrumental in turning our dreams into reality," says the client.

When a client wanted to sell his advertising agency, Clear Vision's founder Rob Walsh:

- Saved everybody a lot of stress, uncertainty and hard work by lining up two of its senior managers, Alice and Ann, to buy it

- Mediated in the negotiations

- Showed them how to raise the finance

- Helped them articulate their vision for the business going forward, and create a business structure that would deliver that vision

- Assisted them in making the transition from managers to owners

- Ran and continues to run regular board meetings, to keep them focused on the key numbers and the key actions

- Provided much needed reassurance throughout the whole process. "What really helped," explains Alice, "is that he spoke to us as families, as well as from a business perspective, he really understood what everyone was putting into it, both financially and emotionally."

The results have been very impressive:

- "It's a completely different agency. As I sit here I can hear laughter down in the studio. That's never happened before, and is a really big thing for me," says Ann.

- "Initially it all felt extremely daunting. But thanks to the structure, guidance and input Clear Vision has given to us I always come out of our board meetings feeling happy, focused, lighter and with a drive to conquer the next three months until we meet again," she adds.

- That input, vision, focus and drive has made the business even more financially successful than anyone anticipated – and as a result they have been able to complete the buyout in two years rather than the expected three.

Alice explains, "what made it all work so well was having someone who actually cares about the future of the business, our strategy and our personal goals, as well as our business goals. I didn't know all of that was possible from accountants, as I thought it was just a numbers thing. But now I realise it's much more than that."

Ann puts it even more succinctly: "Having a really good accountant has been instrumental in turning our dreams into reality."

Restoring the health and happiness of an exhausted business owner

Clear Vision, a two director practice based in a market town in Wiltshire, England, has helped a business owner:

- Transform her health
- Liberate her from having to do everything personally
- Enjoy work again

"I'm actually a new person. Very positive, very calm, and in a very, very good place," says the client.

Janine Greyling had built a very successful recruitment company. But she was doing almost everything herself, there was constant stress and pressure, and as a result, "I was waking up in the morning feeling tired, coming to work tired, going to bed tired, gaining weight massively and my health was going down the drain. So I got to a point where I decided things couldn't go on that way."

At that point she turned to Clear Vision, who helped:

- **Set her goals** – "My main goal was losing weight. I couldn't keep on gaining weight and feeling tired because I was gaining weight."

- **Develop an action plan** – The Vision Day, facilitated by Clear Vision, at which Janine's goals were identified, also resulted in a detailed action plan to support and achieve those goals. And that action plan was monitored and updated at regular board meetings that were also facilitated by the practice.

- **Identify her core values** – "We needed to employ people so I wouldn't be forced to do everything myself. But if they were going to work for us, they would have to understand our core values, and that meant those core values needed to be written down very carefully."

- **Establish clear reporting lines** – "They made me understand the vital importance of being crystal clear on who reports to who, and helped me to put those reporting lines in place, so that I can delegate secure in the knowledge of who will be reporting back to me."

- **Implement daily team meetings** – "This was one of the most important pieces in the puzzle, because it provided a forum for addressing problems, and gave me the peace of mind I needed in order to feel comfortable in delegating."

The impact has been genuinely life changing for Janine. "For the first time I've been able to go on holiday. I've lost a lot of weight and I'm actually a new person. Very positive, very calm, and in a very, very good place. And it's great to get out of bed and go to work knowing that I'm really going to enjoy the day."

Virtual Chief Financial Officer support helps create a $5 million start up

Collins Hume is a five partner practice with two offices in New South Wales, Australia, that has helped a client:

- Start up in the face of a slump in their industry
- Grow to $5 million in 24 months
- Create work and income for the families of 36 team members and contractors

"Having an accountant who shares their values works brilliantly well for them and for us," says one of the firm's partners.

Collins Hume's partner Peter Fowler provides a Virtual Chief Finance Officer service to a project management company in the construction industry. His input has helped the company grow from being a start-up to $5 million of turnover in its first 24 months of trading. The business also uses the services of six employees and over 30 contractors, helping many families to weather the storm in the construction industry.

Some of the key ways they have helped include:

- **Facilitating a strategic planning workshop** – which identified the three key roles that were needed in the business, and how the strengths of the key people could be best used in those roles. As a result, one of the founders concentrates on the client facing and project management activities. The other founder uses her corporate talents to streamline the backend, formally document policies and systems and give overall structure to their venture. And Collins Hume earns a substantial fee for acting as the Virtual CFO.

- **Recommending business books** – including the change management primer 'Who Ate My Cheese' that, according to the client "really set us on a path to establishing business practices that were pivotal to our decision making and ensuring that we could embrace change."

- **Setting up a Self Managed Superannuation Fund** – and using this pension vehicle to buy a commercial office warehouse which can then be rented back to the business. The client explains, "As well as having a property asset for the future, it means we are employing more options now which are benefiting us for the future. It also gives us diversity and room to grow. Having room for growth was important to us."

- **Regular meetings** – "Focusing on strategic planning, creating a one page performance strategy, devising their business scorecard, setting targets, monitoring their financial and non-financial key performance indicators, obsessing about cash flow management, developing policies and systems, always considering the tax planning angles and holding everyone accountable until the next meeting, has made an enormous difference to bedding in best practice early on," explains Peter.

The client puts it this way: "We are fairly conservative when it comes to taking risks, so won't jump without proper planning. We needed an accountant who shared our values, which Peter does."

"Having an accountant who shares their values," explains Peter, "works brilliantly well for them and for us, because they have just renewed the Virtual CFO arrangement for another 12 months, and set a new target of becoming a $10 million business in two years."

Quadrupling the overseas presence of a world-class butcher

Costmasters is a firm with a team of six in Brussels, Belgium that has helped a client to:

- Quadruple their presence in Brussels
- Implement state-of-the-art internal controls
- Reinforce their international reputation

"Without our input it would all have been so much more difficult and risky for them," says Costmasters' founder.

The O'Shea family have been high quality Irish butchers since the 18th century. By 2013 one of their descendants, Jack O'Shea, had established his own shops in London and Brussels, and had built an international reputation for excellence. Since starting to work with Costmasters, however, his Brussels presence has quadrupled, adding two new shops and an extremely successful Chophouse restaurant.

Costmasters' founder, Charles Markowicz, comes from a retailing family and has a background in internal audit, both of which have proved invaluable to this client. According to Charles, some of the main ways they made a difference included:

1. **Sorting out the balance sheet** – "Due to differences between UK and Belgian GAAP, the balance sheet was in a poor state and presented a misleading picture. If we hadn't corrected it quickly the Belgian authorities would probably have invoked their right to assume that the accounts were wrong until the client could prove otherwise. That would have been an enormous distraction at a time when they needed to focus on growth. So correcting the balance sheet, and making sure it didn't go wrong again, was a key initial priority," explains Charles.

2. **Restructuring the accounts function** – "To give them up-to-date and accurate management information, we took over their accounting and streamlined large parts of it by automating the posting of bank feeds, and scanning purchase invoices directly into the accounts."

3. **Obtaining grant funding** – They also helped Jack O'Shea obtain 50% grant funding towards the cost of consultancy support provided by Costmasters.

4. **Implementing electronic tills** – "The grant funding allowed us to research and implement the very best electronic till solution for them, interviewing suppliers and even spending a day visiting a butcher 60 km away to see it working in practice."

5. **Introducing robust internal controls** – "Due to my background in retailing, I knew that running multiple sites is very much more demanding than just one. Because the owner can't physically be at all of the sites, all of the time, you need much tighter internal controls to ensure that cash and stock don't go missing. So that is what we have set up for them. For example, the electronic till system we implemented means that only the manager in each location ever actually touches any cash."

Charles adds, "Quadrupling the size of your business in 12 months is never easy. Doing it overseas is even harder. But Jack O'Shea has achieved that, and their Brussels operations are now even more successful than the original business in London. Most of that success is, of course, down to the fact that they are world-class at what they do. But I also know that without our input it would all have been so much more difficult and risky for them. So we are really proud to have played our part in creating something very special."

Preventing a community from losing something that really matters to them

Excel Partners is a four member team based in Dublin, Ireland that has helped a not-for-profit community organisation:

- Avoid bankruptcy
- Restructure and reduce its debts
- Prevent an invaluable sports and community centre disappearing

"And all without charging anything for their support and expertise."

"Donegal is one of the most economically challenged areas in Europe, caught in an economic pincer of high unemployment and low incomes," explains Excel Partners' Sean Carr. To help redress this, in 2008 a concerted local campaign led to the creation of the Kerrykeel Park and Community Centre. It provides state-of-the-art facilities, and is especially popular with the 70 young children who attend the Sunday morning soccer academy, while its meeting rooms are used by community associations ranging from the tidy town committee to young mothers groups.

But by late 2014 the not-for-profit community committee running it was seriously worried. As Sean explains, "The facility had suffered serious flood damage, their borrowings were enormous and they were facing the prospect of losing everything."

Stepping in on a pro bono basis, Sean and his team were able to:

- Break a two year deadlock in the negotiations with the lender

- Secure a "standstill period" to give them time to identify a solution

- Assess the future viability

- Formulate a comprehensive plan to turn things around

- Prepare a detailed debt mediation restructuring proposal and cost benefit analysis which demonstrated that if a consensual restructuring was undertaken it would result in maximising the return to lender.

As a result, and without charging anything for their support and expertise, Excel Partners were able to:

• Get a significant part of the debt written off

• Prevent the community organisation from bankruptcy

• Save the entire facility for the benefit of local people

"I have operated on many multi-million euro corporate finance and restructuring deals, but this assignment is the most important and best deal I have been involved with," says Sean.

And the Donegal community seem to share that sentiment, since they have unveiled a plaque in honour of the Excel Partners team, which is thought to be the only one of its kind anywhere in the world.

Lifting the fog and avoiding catastrophic job losses

HTA Advisory, a two partner firm with a team of 15 based in Cremorne, Australia, helped a client to:

- Cope with a dramatic fall in sales caused by the global financial crisis
- Improve productivity and reduce costs
- Avoid catastrophic job losses
- Take back control of the business

"Now the fog has lifted... and the future looks bright. So he is relieved, grateful and very happy," says partner Tim Hale.

As innovators in the field of environmentally friendly solutions, ABC's services (name changed to protect their confidentiality) were seen as "nice to have", rather than "essential", and so demand dropped dramatically during the global financial crisis.

HTA partner Tim Hale explains, "after they were referred to us we very quickly identified how we could make the greatest difference." After gaining their trust, by listening and making sure they really understood the business, HTA:

- **Improved performance** – by putting ABC through the practice 's monthly management advisory programme that identified each of the key drivers in the business, and systematically working on improving them.

- **Reduced overhead costs by $30,000 a year** – "At the time he was operating through two shop fronts with a top heavy management team. So we put a proposal forward to merge the two shops and address numerous efficiency problems we had identified in the service delivery method."

- **Improved productivity by 10% in 12 months** – by developing a set of key performance indicators that allowed management to identify the specific processes, systems and team members that were underperforming.

- **Overhauled their reporting** – by implementing two integrated cloud-based systems that allow them to automate large parts of data entry, review the performance of every job against budget, forecast revenues accurately, plan workflow efficiently and make it possible for the owner to understand and control the financial side of the business.

Tim adds, "At a time when a big increase in sales wasn't an option, this focus on operations, costs, efficiency and financial clarity has made the difference between survival and insolvency with catastrophic job losses."

"At the start our client was very nervous, and was effectively 'running blind' using a reporting system that did not help him understand why his business model wasn't profitable, or what to do about it. But now the fog has lifted. The numbers make sense to him, he is back in control, the business is stable, and the future looks bright. So he is relieved, grateful and very happy. And he regularly turns to us for business advice, treating us as a key part of his team."

Taking a huge weight off a client's shoulders

Jason Blackman, a sole practitioner from Lewes, England, has helped a client to:

- Stop worrying about the financial side of her social enterprise
- Save "unprecedented" amounts of time and effort
- Give dozens of disadvantaged people a fresh start in life

"The huge weight I felt has entirely lifted and I feel so much more confident and happy about our business moving forward," says the client.

Enterprise Exchange is a small social enterprise that specialises in helping offenders, ex-offenders, the long-term unemployed and others who are struggling to start a business.

"Our accounting system was antiquated, taking up a huge amount of time and costing us a fortune, but still not giving us the information we needed," explains director Benna McCartney. "And things had got so bad that our future was hanging in the balance."

According to Benna the key things Jason Blackman of Just Pure did to help were:

- **Taking away the stress** – "Jason was open, honest, down-to-earth, calm and friendly. At our first meeting he made me feel completely at ease, spoke to me like a 'human being', and made it very clear (in layman's terms) exactly what needed doing to sort out the current situation."

- **Sorting out the problems** – "In no time he had reviewed and sorted everything, setting us up with a FreeAgent accounting system and Receipt Bank to automate large parts of our processing. It has made it all so easy for us, and we now get the information we need, with much less cost and effort."

- **Listening** – "I feel I can talk to him about everything and anything. He has become a friend and someone I can really trust with my business, which is such a new and exciting experience for me."

- **Helping the wider stakeholder base** – "Unbelievably, he also went out of his way to create a complete accounting package specifically for our clients! This has changed the lives of dozens of people, who I honestly believe would not have survived in the business world for more than five minutes without it. And it has also taken a massive amount of pressure off our work with these particular clients, which has saved us time and money too."

"At the beginning I found our accounting experience really stressful and was extremely worried about our business moving forward," says Benna.

"The amount of time, energy and effort Jason has saved us is unprecedented. The huge weight I felt has entirely lifted and I feel so much more confident and happy in our business moving forward. More than anything, it means I can focus on what is really important in the business, without having to worry about the financial side whatsoever."

Jason himself says, "From a technical perspective, we didn't really do anything difficult. But the point is that what we accountants see as fairly ordinary advice and support can often make an EXTRAORDINARY difference to the businesses, lives and happiness of our clients. The profession has so much more power to do good than it gives itself credit for. That power is at our fingertips. And thanks to new technology, such as cloud accounting and everything that goes with it, our power to make a difference is getting greater and greater by the day."

Creating financial security for the founder of a business and his entire extended family

A two director practice with a team of 15 based in Reading, England that helped a client:

- Pass control of the business he founded over to his son
- Create financial security for himself and his entire extended family
- Save £1 million of tax in the process

"As well as making life better for our client's entire family, this exercise earned us our largest ever fee. And because what we did is so replicable, we now offer it as a packaged service to all of our clients," says the practice's managing director.

Kirkpatrick and Hopes has developed a new kind of "Income and Share Ownership Planning" (ISOP) approach to succession planning, which has become central to their marketing differentiation strategy. And their managing director, Andrew Gray, has even written the book "Do More of What You Love" about it.

Andrew explains, "What makes our ISOP service unique is that it allows our clients to turn a large part of the value they have created in the business into cash, set up their family or key team members to take the business forward, and still allow the client to carry on being involved doing the things they love most in the business. So it's a kind of best of both worlds solution for everyone. And for many people that is a very attractive alternative to selling the business and being left with a sense of emptiness and guilt."

The proof of concept for the ISOP approach came when Kikpatrick and Hopes used it to help the founder of a very profitable £5 million turnover business to:

- Engineer an exit route that resulted in him saving £700k in tax by creating a Newco that allowed him to benefit from Entrepreneurs Relief.

- Create financial security for his extended family by giving them shares in the Newco, on which they earn dividends (this dividend approach also saves the family further tax of £75,000 a year).

- Empower his son to run the business and take it to new levels.

- Make it possible for other key employees to become shareholders and future owners of the business.

"It also meant that the founder can now take more of a back seat role. Still getting involved in the things he loves, but also having much more time for all the other things that are important to him. Unsurprisingly, his initial feeling of frustration at not knowing what to do to keep everybody happy has now been replaced by a sense of relief and delight at getting it sorted in a way that gives everybody what they want, and saves them around £1 million in tax in the process.

"We project-managed the whole exercise, bringing in solicitors, financial advisers etc. to deal with every aspect of the plan," says Andrew. "As a result we also earned £59,000 for the initial work (the biggest single invoice we have ever raised), and now earn £36,000 a year for all the ongoing work. So it was a brilliant outcome for us too."

Preventing a client losing his business and his family home

A two director practice with a team of 14 based in Watford, England helped a client to:

- Turn losses of £350,000 into profits of £650,000
- Avoid losing his business and his house
- Save £260,000 in tax

Director Paul Meades says: "It feels great to have been able to help prevent that kind of catastrophe for our client and his family. And, as you can imagine, our client feels great too."

Within three years of being appointed, Meades & Company had helped this waste recycling business:

- Turn losses of £350,000 into profits of £650,000

- Transform its balance sheet from £850,000 net liabilities into £1.4 million of net assets

- Replace £300,000 of bank borrowings with cash balances of £650,000

- Save the business owner £260,000 in tax

Paul Meades explains: "The owner moved to us after I demonstrated how we could initially save him £16,000 in personal tax a year. But it soon became clear that they needed our all-inclusive service giving them monthly management accounts, management information, ratio analysis, cash flow and profit forecasts and KPI monitoring, along with all the normal year-end accounts payable and tax returns support.

"Armed with that kind of meaningful, reliable and insightful information, we have held monthly BoardView strategic meetings with the owner, helping him use the data to identify and address the areas of the business that needed improving. Acting as a sounding board, and helping him make better decisions based on better information, has proved invaluable to a client who historically had only ever worked 'in', rather than 'on' his business.

"Most importantly, the bank has told us that in the early days they were only able to continue to support the business because of the very comprehensive management information we provided on a regular basis, and twice yearly projected profit and loss accounts, balance sheets and cash flow forecasts. Without that bank support, the owner would probably have lost his business and his house. So it feels great to have been able to help prevent that kind of catastrophe for our client and his family. And, as you can imagine, our client feels great too."

Restoring harmony in a family business

A two partner practice with three team members in Illinois, USA, that has helped a client to:

- Bring a tricky family succession issue out into the open
- Reduce the client's stress levels and restore family harmony

"Our client is now actually excited."

A client had successfully built a business worth $10 million. But he suddenly asked for an emergency meeting, and brought his family along. The client and his wife were extremely stressed, because their children didn't seem to want to step up to take over the business. "After three very difficult hours, and a lot of family grievances being aired, the fog started to lift," partner Jody Padar explained. "We certainly hadn't found a solution by then. But our client was much happier now that everyone had acknowledged that there was a problem, and that it was out in the open.

"This is still a work in progress project, and we still haven't found a perfect succession solution. But our client is now actually excited – and I use that word deliberately – that the issue is being addressed. As accountants we often don't appreciate the enormous difference we can make just by bringing people together and encouraging them to get their issues out onto the table. That alone can be profoundly valuable to them. Of course, the ultimate solution may involve bringing in outside experts, but often all we need to do is facilitate things.

"A key insight for us", says Jody, "is that many of our other clients may well be feeling the same way. So rather than wait for them to come to us in desperation, we intend to design a system the entire team can use to identify the early warning signs. And the great thing about harnessing cloud technology is that it frees up the time we need to be able to be a lot more proactively valuable, in this and other ways, to a lot more of our clients."

Unleashing the potential of a junior employee

Pearson Buchholz is a 25 person practice in Oxford, England that has helped a junior credit controller:

- Transform and take over the entire accounting function at a 35 person business
- Get promoted to the management team
- Make life much less stressful for the business owner

"There is often so much untapped potential in people. And by giving it a chance to flourish we can make things better for everyone," says their Business Services Director.

Ian Woollard first met Sarah Fenwick, the founder of energy assessment company Energis UK Limited, when she was the guest speaker at a networking supper. "She was trying to run a 35 employee business using information that was out of date and a struggle to obtain," explains Ian.

"So we replaced their antiquated systems, and a raft of outsourced suppliers, with a single all-encompassing cloud based accounting solution that could be used perfectly by the in-house team. And that was made possible because very early on we identified an absolute gem of a member of staff, Jo.

"Jo had been employed simply as a credit controller, and was instrumental in helping me transform everything. My role was to lead the project, and work with her for the next six months to help her take over, monitoring her progress along the way. And as part of that, Jo and I sat down for two hours a month doing an analytical review of the numbers to anticipate Sarah's questions and identify problem solving suggestions in advance. "

The results have been impressive:

- Jo now leads the entire accounting function, has been given a pay rise, promoted to the management team, and has started studying for professional exams

- The conversion to the new system has been successfully completed

- The entire management accounting process has been systemised and documented – making month ends quick and smooth

- In addition, eliminating the need for outsourced suppliers has saved them a considerable amount of time and money

"Sarah used to be frustrated and annoyed by the finance side of the business. But now all that stress has been removed because she has the reliable and timely information she needs to properly understand what is happening, make better decisions and drive the business forward.

"The really inspiring thing for me personally, though, is to see the development of Jo from a credit controller to a trusted senior manager in 12 short months. Don't get me wrong, she is incredibly hard-working and really deserves her chances. But to see such a remarkable progress will stick with me for a long time. And it has taught me to look far deeper into people. Far deeper than simply looking at what they currently do, but to really understand what drives them, and why they do what they do.

"There is often so much untapped potential in people. And by giving it a chance to flourish we can make things better for everyone. So I am now actively and deliberately looking for the Jo in every client I work with."

Making accountancy fun

This three-person, employee-owned bookkeeping practice in Ashland, Oregon, USA was named as a Firm of the Future by Intuit because it is:

- Making accountancy fun and approachable
- Pioneering the AskABookkeeper.com video series
- Giving clients permission to love their businesses again

"After all, if you don't enjoy it, what's the point?" says the firm's founder.

"When QuickBooks Online transitioned to the new Harmony version our clients were lost," says Polymath's founder Ingrid Edstrom. "So we created a 13-part QuickBooks Online tutorial series to bridge the gap. Since then, we have continued to develop our video library to help many business owners and accounting professionals free of charge."

One of those developments has been to launch puppet mascots for the practice, and feature them in an innovative new series of videos. "Basically we are creating 'Sesame Street' for business owners," says Ingrid. "It's still a fairly new project for us, so while only a handful of videos are currently online, we have more than a dozen currently in production, and we come up with new creative ideas every day.

"The main puppet, who represents the average micro-business owner, is 'Penny the Practical Professional.' She runs a very small pie shop which she started because she loves baking and wanted to support herself with her 'art.' She promptly realized that running a business was not as easy for her as making pies, and she found herself getting stuck in every pitfall imaginable. The worst of those pitfalls was her 'Paper Monster,' which is represented by our second puppet mascot, 'Polly the Paper Monster.' And over the course of her story Penny learns that she can defeat her paper monster by using software to keep things organized.

"We are also working on a third puppet, 'Procrastinator Gator.' This fun character has a difficult time because he keeps putting off the administrative portions of running his business. But with a little help from us, he changes his habits and becomes the 'Dele-Gator.'

"We grab people's attention by making it fun. But it is fun with a very serious intent, because we use the puppets to help clients:

- Identify and tackle the issues holding them back
- Take full advantage of cloud and other technology to make their businesses run more smoothly, efficiently and profitably
- Make their businesses leverageable and ready for growth
- Lead from a place of knowledge and power, and delegate from a position of strength, rather than abdicating when they feel like they're losing control.

"Often clients come to us feeling completely overwhelmed," says Ingrid. "They feel ashamed about how bad they have allowed their situation to get, and often they break down into tears in our office. That is when we remind them that our tag-line is 'A Weight Off Your Shoulders' for very good reasons.

"But soon their relief is clear. They are so happy to be delegating the things that they don't enjoy so that they can focus on their dreams again. We all started our businesses because we wanted to support our lives doing something that we love. So we give them permission to love their business again. After all, if you don't enjoy it, what's the point?

"By helping our clients in these ways, we are also creating jobs, and improving the lives of their teams, customers, children and families. And our videos are also helping accountants and bookkeepers across the world be more approachable, and do a better job. So we are improving the economy and the world through bookkeeping, one business at a time.

"We were also thrilled to be named by Intuit as a 'Firm of The Future' in 2015. We strongly believe that the accountants of the future must be creative, personable, professional, passionate, and have hungry minds that are eager to stay on the cutting edge of technology. They must also make our industry more welcoming and approachable to the average business person. And that is exactly our vision for Polymath."

Helping clients to live without regrets, so they can die without regrets

RJS Accounting, a single partner firm with 7 team members in Queensland, Australia, that helps clients to:

- Build businesses they love
- Live life without regrets, so they can die without regrets
- Get the perfect work-life balance

"It can be a tricky balance, of course. But it's probably the most valuable and important thing any accountant can do for their clients," says the firm's owner.

There are moments in life that change everything. And Kylie Anderson, who runs RJS, had one of them 10 years ago.

"My life changed dramatically when my husband suddenly died. We were both young, and it had a profound impact on my view of the world. I used to be a typically boring accountant who focused on saying negative things like 'you can't afford that', and 'you must save your money for retirement.'

"But now, while I still talk to my clients about the importance of saving and planning for the future, I also tell them that they have to live for today because none of us has any idea of what's around the corner.

"It's the philosophy I live by. I travel when I want to. I work when I want to. I do what I love. And I absolutely live my life, because I believe that if you live without regrets, you die without regrets.

"And that's now the philosophy and focus for our business too. We want to help clients get to a position of loving what they do. Creating businesses that they love and enjoy going to. But that they can also get away from when they want to. So they can go on their holidays, lead their lives and get the whole work-life balance thing perfect. And all without getting grief from an accountant who says negative things like, 'you shouldn't be spending that money on holidays and enjoying yourself!'"

"The bottom line is that we don't want miserable clients.

"In the past, we saw too many people save all their money for retirement. And then something drastic happened, and they never got the chance to enjoy the fruits of all that hard work.

"So all our clients know that they can come to us and say, 'I want to blow $10,000 on a holiday', and we'll say, 'OK, let's see how we can make that happen for you.' At the same time as helping them to be responsible and save for retirement.

"It can be a tricky balance, of course. But it's probably the most valuable and important thing any accountant can do for their clients. Because that way we can help them to live lives without regret."

Winning national awards and international recognition by reinventing the business model

Sky Accountants is a three office, 14 person firm based in the Melbourne area of Australia that has helped its founder:

- Go on a journey from suicidal thoughts to personal fulfilment
- Achieve all of his dreams by the age of 30
- Build a business that is winning national awards and international recognition

"Sky Accountants has given me back the time I needed to achieve all of those dreams I set for myself in my darkest hour... And that is simply priceless," says the founder.

Sky Accountants founder and CEO, Jamie Johns, has been on quite a journey. "At 16 I was struggling at school, partly because I am dyslexic, and was close to committing suicide. But I didn't do it, and instead I focused on the positives by writing down my dreams for my life. Looking back now, I believe that I had achieved every one of those dreams by the time I was 30."

It certainly wasn't all plain sailing. "Five years ago I got fed up with my practice. I was working without a vision or goal. I was working too hard, which wasn't sustainable. Some of the people around me were pulling me backwards. And I knew that when I was on my death bed I didn't want to look back and say 'if only'."

"So after some life-changing coaching from Rob Nixon and Colin Dunn, I sold my shares in the old business and re-invented a completely new one, calling it Sky Accountants because my favourite saying had always been 'the sky's the limit'."

Everything about the new Sky Accountants business model is different from the way Jamie used to operate:

- The entire business is run from the cloud using tools such as Xero Practice Management, NowInfinity, Class Super, SharePoint, Harmon. ie and their own in-house built software, Scorecard. "This allows us to schedule all our work clearly, collect information upfront, process jobs faster and add more value than almost every other accountant."

- All work is done on a fixed-fee and value-based basis, with payment upfront.

- All of their services have been productised, with a four tier (Bronze, Silver, Gold and Platinum) pricing structure, "so that we never leave money on the table."

- Their guarantees include, "Unlike some accountants who see phone calls and emails as rich pickings, we don't charge them as extra."

- They outsource the 'grinding' work to a couple of accountants based in the Philippines, one of whom lived with Jamie and his team for four weeks to get her up to speed.

- And they offer a high-end business mentoring program powered by a 7 module written course.

"This approach has literally changed my life as well as my business," says Jamie. Those life changing results include:

- **Attracting high quality dynamic clients** – the largest of which turns over $30 million.

- **Dramatic growth** – including opening two new offices (one physical, the other virtual).

- **Peer recognition** – including being featured in Xero's 2015 roadshow across Australia, working for the Institute of Public Accountants to teach other professionals how to follow in his footsteps and being a columnist for Accountants Daily, where he regularly ranks at the top of the discussion comments.

- **Specialisation** – leading the firm to now specialise in hospitality and tourism.

- **Winning a major award** – in 2015 Sky Accountants were named by Panalitix as Australia's Most Innovative Accounting Firm, and they were also shortlisted as a finalist by Accountants Daily as The Most Innovative Firm in Australia.

"What's even more important to me," Jamie explains, "is that Sky Accountants has given me the opportunity to achieve all of those dreams I set for myself in my deepest and darkest hour when I was 16. Some kids just don't return from the feeling of hopelessness. The biggest thing to take away from my life so far is that anything is possible for those who have an insane persistence to follow their heart and dreams. The key is to never stop searching for your niche in life and never give up."

Leveraging the trusted adviser status of accountants

A South African accountant on a mission to help thousands of clients by:

- Providing a one-stop-shop solution that builds on the accounting profession's unique status as trusted advisers
- Sharing what he has learned with the entire profession

"By leveraging our trusted adviser status, we accountants can make more of a difference than ever before."

Erick Liebenberg is an accountant with vision. For 20 years he has been in public practice and now leads this five partner practice. While others talk about the trusted adviser status of accountants, his guiding principle has always been to design his entire business model around it.

His vision involves seeing the accountant-client relationship as a portal through which businesses can access everything they need. Erick envisioned a firm that has the ability to address most, if not all, of the financial services and advisory needs of individuals and businesses alike: "to increase their stakeholder's profits, their business' value and personal wealth by grouping various professionals under one proverbial roof."

So he created a group of 16 independent companies that trade under one brand, The Core Group.

Each of those companies specialises in providing one key type of help, including training, insurance, business coaching, risk management, valuations, IT support, HR and even brand management, alongside the more traditional cloud accounting, auditing, tax planning and financial services solutions.

Erick explains, "our clients love the fact that we have taken the one-stop-shop idea, and made it a valuable reality for them. As a result our relationships with our clients are now deeper rooted than ever before.

And because they procure so many more services through us, those relationships have become more profitable."

That is only the half of the story though. "After 11 years of dreaming, then nine years of testing the model on our own practice, and two years of packaging it, we decided it's time to take the model national. In August 2015 we rolled out everything we have learnt to the entire accounting profession here in South Africa," states Erick.

"Within a couple of months 11 other practices had started to plug into our one-stop-shop model, by using The Core Group branding, systems, tool and solutions. Already more than 5000 of their clients (who also become new clients to us) can now benefit from the help provided by the 16 Core Group companies. This is just the beginning, because within the next six years we expect to be making a difference to 200 accounting practices and over 100,000 of their clients. By leveraging our trusted adviser status in this manner, we accountants can make more of a difference than ever before."

Creating four new jobs and the time and money to pursue a passion

Sole practitioner with a team of 10 in Ashby-de-la Zouch, England that has helped a client to:

- Double profits
- Move to bigger and better premises
- Create four new jobs
- Transform his work life balance

"He is now much happier, and so are his family."

Dean started his forklift truck business in 2003. Ten years later he was working long days, late nights and weekends, and was often forced to sacrifice holidays, all to make a modest profit.

Ian Rodgers, The Profit Key's founder, explains, "As our name suggests, we specialise in helping businesses become more profitable. So we started having regular Business One Page Plan meetings with Dean. And the key to improving his profits soon became obvious: because he was personally at full stretch, the only way to grow was to employ another engineer. Unfortunately he wasn't willing to spend the money employing someone until the business grew. So, because he became locked in a 'chicken and egg' stalemate, nothing got better and the meetings stopped.

"A year later we met to finalise his annual accounts, which once again only showed modest profits. At that meeting I crunched the numbers to show him once again how little in extra sales he would need to get a payoff from employing another engineer. And this time the penny dropped. So Dean asked for the Business One Page Plan meetings to be restarted, because if he was going to 'risk' hiring more people he wanted the confidence and control of being close to all the key performance numbers."

Ian now gets well paid for sitting down with Dean every month to:

- Monitor performance by reviewing all the key numbers that matter to the business

- Build on what is working well

- Take corrective action to improve the things that aren't working well

- Make people accountable so that the things on the action plan actually get done

Within a year the impact was dramatic. "Profits have doubled, they've moved to bigger and better premises, and four new jobs have been created. Even better than all of that, taking on new people means that Dean no longer has to do everything himself. So he now has much more time for his young family. And he has the time and money to really get stuck into his passion for off-road enduro motorbike racing. So, as you can imagine, he is now much happier, and so are his family."

Making life better for 8 million people

Accountants Changing the World is a not-for-profit movement that has:

- Inspired 154 accountants in 8 countries
- Helped over 8 million people in need across the world

"I believe that helping to make things better is what life is all about," says the movement's founder.

This chapter has been kept separate from the alphabetical order of the other inspirational stories for two reasons. Firstly, because it is different in nature and structure. Secondly, and more importantly, because it features one of the book's authors, and we didn't want to appear to be showing favouritism by putting it alphabetically at the front of the book.

Accountants Changing the World ('ACTW') was launched as a non-for-profit movement in 2012 to help UK accountants in practice to make the world a better place.

To the uninitiated, the idea that ordinary accountants can change the world might sound absurd. But, as the stories in this book prove, it is happening all the time. And ACTW gives accountants a suite of free tools to make it even easier.

Why

The movement's founder, Steve Pipe, explains, "This is why I get up every morning. You see, I believe that helping to make things better is what life is all about. And as accountants we are uniquely equipped to do it."

How

Of course, it's not about grand gestures, posturing or pretending to be some kind of superhero.

Instead it's about accountants using their professional and business skills to do lots of simple little things. Each of which makes a small (and sometimes not so small) difference.

Doing them really well, with passion, energy and skill. And doing them alongside many other accountants who share these beliefs and passion. So that together, one tiny step at a time, things get a little bit better for the thousands of people and businesses we collectively help.

Together all those little things add up. They really do.

In fact, by the end of January 2016 the 154 accountants and practices who have officially become "Accountants Changing the World" signatories had collectively already made things better in meaningful ways for 8,057,019 people (you can see the up to date number at accountantschangingtheworld.com).

What

Becoming an ACTW signatory involves making three formal commitments:

- **Commitment 1: Tackling economic stagnation** – helping businesses create more prosperity, wealth and jobs for themselves and the wider economy – and one of the ways they honour this commitment is by offering every business in their area a free Profit Improvement Review.

- **Commitment 2: Reducing global warming** – helping businesses cut their costs by reducing their carbon footprint so that the world is kept safe for future generations – and one of the ways they honour this part of their commitment is by offering every business in their area a free Sustainability Audit.

- **Commitment 3: Alleviating poverty and suffering** – helping businesses to flourish by giving them more energy and purpose by connecting at deeper level with the good causes they support – and one of the ways they honour this part of their commitment is by offering every business in their area a free Social Responsibility Review.

The three commitments aren't in any way legally binding, since ACTW is a voluntary movement. Instead, they are a statement of intent, and are driven by integrity.

ACTW provides signatories with all the free resources, free tools, free software and free support they need in order to be able to honour these commitments. For example, signatories receive benchmarking software that allows them to show businesses their strengths and weaknesses and use the insights to develop a profit improvement action plan.

Whilst not compulsory, ACTW also encourages signatories to change the world for talented 18-25 year olds by giving them work experience and/ or internships during which they actually do much of the work involved in honouring the commitments listed above.

NOTE: ACTW was originally created for UK accountants. The free resources, tools, software and support it provides are therefore UK-centric. However, its signatories now also include accountants in South Africa, the USA, Australia, India, Egypt, Uganda and Canada, who have used them as the inspiration for their own approaches to honouring the spirit of the three commitments.

The benefits

Firms become signatories because it "feels right". In the broadest possible sense, they know it is the right thing to do. Once they become involved, however, they discover that their involvement also gives them profound emotional and commercial benefits.

"At an emotional level, making a genuine difference in all these ways is joyful, uplifting and inspiring," explains Steve. "It gives the entire practice a greater sense of purpose, a greater source of energy, and a greater feeling of happiness. And it brings practitioners, their teams and their families an immense feeling of pride."

While at a commercial level, ACTW also provides signatories with a full suite of marketing tools to help them:

- Build an outstanding reputation as a practice that really cares and really does make a difference

- Receive more referrals – because of this enhanced reputation

- Generate even more sales leads – because of the free profit improvement reviews, free sustainability audits and free social responsibility reviews

- Attract high quality clients and team members who are inspired by what they do.

"So, in a very real sense," explains Steve, "signatory firms are also changing their own worlds for the better."

Free help from the authors

Free implementation resources

We have created a suite of free implementation resources to accompany this book. They have not been included within the book itself so that we can keep them up to date and relevant to you regardless of when you are reading this.

So please do ask for the very latest versions by emailing info@avn.co.uk with "WMIA resources' as the subject.

They will help you create an action plan to:

- Inspire your team
- Improve the services you currently offer and the difference you currently make
- Identify and launch new services that will help you to make even more of a difference
- Win better new clients
- Earn better fees
- Obtain tools and support that make it all much easier and quicker

Other free resources that will help you

Although not created specifically to accompany this book, you can also obtain the following additional free resources from the authors to help make your practice even more successful and inspiring:

- **www.improveyourpractice.co.uk** - A free step-by-step programme that gives you world-class training, tools and guidance to help you improve your profits, cashflow, average fees, service levels and client base. Use as much or as little of it as you want. It's all completely free.

- **www.accountantschangingtheworld.com** - A movement and supporting free suite of resources to help you make the world a better place by creating economic growth, reducing environmental damage and addressing the global problem of poverty.

About the authors

Steve Pipe

Steve led the research project. He is a chartered accountant, dynamic keynote speaker, and the founder of both AVN and the Accountants Changing the World movement. In 2012 he was named "The world's most highly rated adviser to accountants" for having more recommendations (now over 480) on LinkedIn than any other adviser. Those recommendations also make him the most highly rated accountant in the world.

His books include "101 ways to make more profits" and "The UK's best accountancy practices". And he is also the creator of the ground-breaking free improveyourpractice.co.uk programme for helping accountants become more profitable by serving clients better than ever before.

He lives in Leeds, England, has been married to an accountant for over 30 years, and in his spare time plays tennis and the blues guitar badly.

Susan Clegg

Susan has spent more than 12 years working with UK accountants, researching what makes them successful, and helping them understand how to build better practices. Her publications include "Everlasting Phone Impressions" and co-authoring "Your blueprint for a better accountancy practice".

She lives in Sheffield, England, has two teenage daughters and loves to write.

Shane Lukas

Shane is the Managing Director of AVN, the UK's leading association of forward thinking proactive accountants. He has probably visited and coached more UK accountants than anyone else, helping them take strides in transforming and improving their accounting practices and consequently their lives. His publications include contributing to "The accountants' essential guide to success".

He is married to an accountant, lives in Derbyshire, England and regularly competes in Iron Man triathlons and Tough Mudder events.

Contacting the authors

All three authors can be contacted via www.avn.co.uk and info@avn.co.uk

The research process

We first came up with the idea for this book in late 2014, and the research for it continued throughout 2015 and into early 2016.

As part of the research, hundreds of thousands of accountants across the world were invited to nominate themselves. This was achieved by:

- Contacting all the c 10,000 accountants we are connected to across the world via email and social media
- Promoting it globally online via articles and blogs on professional community websites such as accountingweb and professional bodies such as the International Federation of Accountants
- Asking leaders within the profession (such as professional bodies, advisers to accountants and other thought leaders) to nominate firms they thought were worthy
- Getting global suppliers to the profession to share the word with their customers and contacts
- Featuring it on stage during conference and exhibition keynote presentations
- Running a competition in the UK to find "The UK's Most Inspiring Accountants" - with the winner chosen by 250 of their peers, and receiving a £10,000 cash prize generously sponsored by Xero

In each case, the process was exactly the same:

- In order to be considered for inclusion, accountants had to tell us one or more story about how they had made a real difference.
- They could do this either by completing a standard written entry form, or via a telephone interview with one of the authors.
- If their story was judged to be sufficiently inspiring, we would write it up as a draft chapter.
- The accountants would then review their draft chapter and request corrections where necessary.
- And in due course, they would confirm in writing that the final version was a true and fair account of this story, and that they (and their client where appropriate) were happy for it to be published.

Only stories that have been confirmed as true and fair in this way are featured in this book.

Thanks and acknowledgements

A project on this scale is only possible with the help and support of a great many people. Firstly, of course, we would like to thank the accountants who shared their stories so openly and candidly with us, including the many who didn't quite make it onto these pages.

Thanks also go to our colleagues at AVN, friends and families who encouraged us at every turn, and to the many professional bodies, suppliers and advisers to accountants who helped us find inspiring stories in their countries. In that latter context, we would like to especially thank Christopher Arnold, Alison Ball, Martin Bissett, Rob Brown, Michael 'MC' Carter, Gale Crossley, Colin Dunn, Paul Dunn, Seth Fineberg, Thea Foster, Amy Harris, Bridgitte Kriel, Steve McIntyre Smith, Mark Lloydbottom, Rob Lovell, Rob Nixon, Edi Osborne, Paul Shrimpling and John Stokdyk.

Finally, our thanks go to Darren Upson, Gary Turner, Ashleigh Lambert and the team at Xero for sponsoring the £10,000 cash prize that kickstarted the research project in the UK.